MOZART

W. A. MOZART

from a woodcut by Eric King

MOZART

by J. E. TALBOT

Great Lives

DUCKWORTH
3 HENRIETTA STREET
LONDON   W.C.2

First published .. 1934
Reprinted .. 1949

Printed in Great Britain by Bristol Typesetting Company
Bristol and London

CONTENTS

CHRONOLOGY

1756   Birth at Salzburg (January 27th).

1763–6 European tour.

1768   First opera.

1769–71 Tour in Italy.

1778   Visit to Munich, Mannheim, and Paris with his mother—her death.

1781   *Idomeneo.*

1781   Leaves Archbishop's service—settles in Vienna.

1782   Meets Haydn—marriage.

1785   Quartets dedicated to Haydn.

1786   *Le Nozze di Figaro.*

1787   Death of Leopold Mozart.

1787   *Don Giovanni.*

1788   Three last symphonies.

1790   *Così fan tutte.*

1791   *Die Zauberflöte — Requiem —* death in Vienna (December 5th).

TO
WALFORD DAVIES

CHAPTER I

A GREY, hard December morning in Salzburg.
Frost had stilled the rushing Salzach, and the
Mönchsberg ridge stood out white and stark
against the heavy clouds. In a little house in the
Getreidegasse preparations for an important
domestic festival were on foot. It was Leopold
Mozart's birthday, and Frau Anna, with the help
of her little daughter Marianne, had been working
from an early hour to get everything into spick
and span order for the party. They were now in
the kitchen, putting the finishing touches to the
birthday feast. Upstairs the four-year-old son of
the house, Wolfgang, was discussing with his
friend, Andreas Schachtner, how they should
while away the hours of waiting. Andreas suggested the game of "school," to which Wolfgang
assented, but only on condition that he took the
part of the master, and that the class was held in
the best sitting-room. A procession was formed,
Wolfgang leading the way with desk and chalk
and Andreas following with a stool. The young
Mozart improvised a marching song for the
occasion, and, to the enlivening strains of his
Opus 1, the boys stamped off in strict time, raising
a cloud of dust as they went. School opened with
an arithmetic lesson, and, as there was no black-

9

board, the teacher chalked up sums and exercises on floor and walls and any piece of furniture that came handy. The lesson was in full swing when Marianne came into the room and gave a cry of horror at the scene that met her eyes. Reproachfully she told Wolfgang of the hours of toil that their mother had spent on tidying and smartening the room, and now there was nothing but mess and confusion, and the work would have to be done all over again. She hurriedly fetched sponge and duster, and did her best to remove all guilty traces of the chalked figures. Her brother looked on ruefully at the work of renovation, then slunk away into a corner of the room to hide his tears, and stood there for some minutes brooding over his misdeeds. A black shadow had crept over his happy day; the bright promise of the morning was wrecked—and it was all his fault. Suddenly the clouds parted outside, a pale gleam of wintry sunlight shot into the room and fell full on the children's favourite canary that had been moping in its cage through the dark days. The bird lifted its head to the light, hopped gaily from perch to perch, and poured forth a full-throated stream of joyous song. Instantly Wolfgang turned and listened; his dull eyes sparkled again, his pale face flushed, every nerve in his body throbbed to the canary's music. All his troubles were forgotten, his game with its tragic ending, his sister's indignant reproof; he was illumined, transformed. Long after the bird's song had ceased and his playfellow had gone home, he stood, motionless, in a blissful trance. At last a gentle touch on his cheek roused him from his dream. It was Marianne, returned with a kiss of forgiveness. He looked up at her with a startled smile, then threw his arms round her neck, and brother and sister were happy again.

The shadows had vanished, and there was nothing now to dull the gaiety of the birthday festivities. When, towards evening, the party at last broke up and the Mozart family were left alone, Leopold, in fulfilment of a long-standing promise, called his daughter to come and have her first lesson on the clavier. She was no stranger to the instrument, and had already acquired a surprising technical facility by hours of surreptitious practising on her own acconut. So now, under her father's guidance, her progress was easy and rapid. As the lesson proceeded, Wolfgang stole up to the clavier, and stood quiet and absorbed at his sister's side. He had often listened to his father's playing without giving it any particular attention; but now, as Marianne's fingers moved deftly over the keys, the little rippling tunes touched his heart, and a voice whispered, "You can do that too." Directly her lesson was over, he jumped on to the stool, and repeated with unerring accuracy the exercises that his sister had been learning. Then he began to delve into the mysteries of harmony, and, with cries of delight, explored the effect of striking two notes together at various intervals. Leopold watched the child's performance with growing astonishment; he felt he was in the presence of genius. He took Wolfgang in his arms and kissed him tenderly; then he made him kneel down by his side and say with him a prayer to the Giver of the great gift, that it might always be used to His glory. The last words of the prayer came slowly and falteringly from the boy's lips; he was tired out, and his eyes were heavy with sleep. His mother carried him off to bed; and, as he laid his head on the pillow and passed into the land of dreams, there floated through his brain sweet memories of the bird's song and messages from the new world of lovely harmony which that day had been revealed to him.

The boy was now dedicated to music, and his powers began to develop with astonishing rapidity. Every day he listened with rapt attention to Marianne's lesson, and it was not long before he persuaded his father to take him on as a regular pupil. He learnt everything that was put before him with incredible ease, and he had soon acquired a considerable repertoire of little pieces, minuets, gavottes, gigues, that he could play by heart. Leopold entered all these in a music-book which had been used for Marianne's exercises, with a careful record of the time that the boy took to learn them. "This minuet and trio," one entry runs, "were learned by little Wolfgang in half-an-hour, at half-past nine at night, on January 26th, 1761, one day before his fifth year."

Wolfgang's working day, it seems, was some-times prolonged beyond the normal bedtime of a five-year-old child. But before its ending, early or late, a little act of evening ritual had always to be performed. The boy would get up on a stool at his father's side and sing with him in two-part harmony a queer jumble of nonsense words to a tune of his own making. This done, he would jump down from the stool, kiss his father on the tip of his nose, give him a solemn promise that he would put him, when he grew old, in a glass case for all the world to honour and revere, and then go off contentedly to bed.

These little evening songs, precursors in minia-ture of "Voi che sapete" and "Batti, batti," have unfortunately not survived; but the young Mozart's promise to confer honour on his father's name has indeed been fulfilled, if not in the precise manner in which the boy expressed it. For Leopold, quick to see in his son unmistakable signs of rare and heaven-sent musical gifts, resolved from the outset to devote his whole strength to the fostering and developing of the boy's artistic powers, and, in the faithful performance of this task to which he gave his life, he obtained a secure, if modest, place among the honoured names of musical history.

He was of humble origin, the son of a bookbinder in Augsburg, a town which a contemporary writer described as "renowned for wig-makers, pits, sulphurous water-works, and dancing ladies." A strange enough list of titles to municipal distinction, and it is not surprising that Leopold should have found the atmosphere of his native town unsympathetic to his studious and serious-minded nature. At any rate he migrated at an early age to Salzburg, and entered the university in that town as a student of jurisprudence. Music, however, was his chief preoccupation; he was a performer of more than average merit on the violin and the organ, and it was not long before he abandoned his legal studies and entered the service of Archbishop Sigismund as court composer and leader of the orchestra. Salzburg was to be his home and the Archbishop his master for the rest of his life; here he married the daughter of the steward of the local convent and became the father of seven children, of whom only two survived their infancy—a girl, Maria Anna, and a boy, four years and a half younger, Wolfgang Amadeus.

In his early days he was an industrious and prolific composer, mainly of Church music, and he enriched the repertoire of the Archbishop's choir with a long series of oratorios, masses, and motets, of blameless mediocrity, and conforming rigidly to the conventional style and idiom of the day.

He also wrote a large number of symphonies, serenades, and concertos, and a set of would-be humorous " occasional pieces " for strange combinations of instruments; and one of Wolfgang's earliest musical memories was that of listening to the band on the city walls playing, at the beginning and end of each day, little tunes by his father with the engaging title—" The Morning and Evening Melodiously and Harmoniously Introduced to the Inhabitants of Salzburg."

The money value of these compositions, however, was no larger than their artistic merit and did little to supplement the miserably small emoluments of a musical post at the Archbishop's court. So Leopold, faced with the expenses of a growing family, was obliged to devote all the time that he could spare from his official duties to giving lessons on the violin and clavier. As a teacher he soon gained a considerable reputation, and in the year of Wolfgang's birth, 1756, he was able to publish, at his own expense, a treatise on the art of violin-playing, which achieved a rapid and wide popularity and laid down the principles on which the best German players of the later eighteenth century modelled themselves. Apart from its technical merits the work is interesting as setting forth the ideals of musical education which Leopold was soon to apply in the training of his son. Thoroughness and hard work, he insists, are the prime requisites in an artist; progress towards technical proficiency must be slow and deliberate; and each piece of ground must be made good before an advance to the next is attempted. Study must be hard and laborious, and the list of exercises given in the book is prefaced by the remark that the more distasteful they are, the better the author will be pleased. The highest degree of natural facility, even genius, in the pupil cannot relieve him from the necessity of arduous technical work; yet the player's technical skill is only the means to a higher end, and that end is the power of expressing, simply and unaffectedly, the full meaning of the music in hand, so as to penetrate to the souls and stir the emotions of those who hear it.

Such was the confession of Leopold's musical faith, and it shows how well qualified he was to guide and guard the wayward steps of genius. To this task he henceforth applied himself with whole-hearted devotion. "God," he wrote to a friend, "has endowed my children with such genius that, not to speak of my duty as a father, my ambition urges me to sacrifice all else to their education." Whatever hopes he may have cherished of personal distinction he laid aside, and, when once he had realized the exceptional musical endowment of his children, he scarcely composed another note. For one gifted with so facile a talent the sacrifice must have been a real one, but it was cheerfully and ungrudgingly made, and for the rest of his life the father resolutely refused to enter into any kind of competition with his son.

CHAPTER II

Wolfgang's childhood—early compositions, and performance —his wonderful ear—sensitiveness—his father's influence.

In the early years of the Mozart children's life it would have been difficult to tell which of the two gave the greater promise of future eminence as a performer. But the boy's mind, unlike his sister's, was from the first occupied with more important things than learning to play other people's music. Very early the creative impulse began to stir within him, and in Marianne's exercise book there are preserved the first essays in composition by the author of *Figaro* and the " Jupiter " symphony. They are in his father's manuscript, taken down as he played them—engaging little pieces, showing already something of the pellucid melody and neatly rounded form which we associate with the name of Mozart.

The young composer, however, even at the age of five, did not always rely on an amanuensis to transcribe his works. One day his father and a friend came upon him busily occupied with pen and ink. He hardly noticed their entrance and went on with his task with concentrated eagerness. They stood and watched him. As each idea came into his head he plunged the pen deep into the very heart of the inkstand. Soon he had covered the paper with huge blots which, as fast as they

16

appeared, he wiped off with the palm of his hand. On this unpromising background was written what at first sight appeared to be an illegible jumble of notes. Wolfgang explained that he was writing a concerto for the clavier, but that it was not finished yet. The two men looked at the blotted music sheet more closely, and gradually it dawned upon them that here was no mere childish nonsense but a genuine piece of musical creation. Leopold, his eyes filling with tears of wonder and delight, drew his friend's attention to the charm of the melodic themes and the clear and orderly structure—" only no use could be made of it," he added, " for it is so immensely difficult that nobody could play it." " That is why it is a concerto," retorted Wolfgang; " it must be practised till it is perfect. Look, it goes something like this "—and the boy jumped on to the clavier stool and plunged eagerly into the opening *allegro*. There was many a stumble over difficult passages, but these were not allowed to interrupt the impetuous flow of the music or to obscure its neat outline. The movement was carried through to a perfectly logical conclusion; then Wolfgang ran up to his father with a happy smile and put the ink-stained score of his first concerto into his hand. Leopold's heart was too full to speak; he laid his hand on the boy's head and gently murmured a blessing. It was the renewed dedication of his son to the service of music.

On his sixth birthday Wolfgang was presented by a friend with a little violin, and at once he set himself to explore the possibilities of the exciting new instrument. He begged his father to give him lessons on it, but Leopold refused, telling him that his clavier practise and composition were quite enough to occupy his time. So there was nothing for it but to see what he could do with the violin by himself. A week or two later a Salzburg violinist, Wenzl by name, came round to the Mozarts' house to try over some string trios that he had just written. Schachtner, chief trumpeter in the private orchestra of the Archbishop and an old friend of the Mozart family, was there, and it was arranged that the composer should play the first violin part in his trio, Schachtner the second, and Leopold the viola. The music was just going to begin when Master Wolfgang came forward with an earnest request that *he* might take the second violin part. Leopold would not hear of this, and though the boy tried to soften his father's heart with the surprising plea that to play second violin no teaching was necessary, it was of no avail, and he was told to go away and not be a nuisance. Sobbing bitterly, Wolfgang slunk out of the room with his little fiddle under his arm. The good Schachtner's heart was touched at this moving spectacle; he interceded with Leopold, and begged that the child might at least be allowed to play the second violin part with him. Leopold agreed to this plan, but only on condition that Wolfgang should play so softly that nobody could hear him. So the trio began. It had not gone far before Schachtner realized with amazement that his little colleague was reading the part with as much assurance and accuracy as himself. He was, after all, quite a superfluous performer; he could leave it all to Wolfgang. So he put down his violin and listened, awestruck. Then he looked at Leopold, and saw that tears were running down his cheeks. The performance was carried through to a success-ful end, and of the occasional mistakes of time or tune that occurred in its course very few were made by the second violin.

Wolfgang's violin studies were now pursued with redoubled zeal. Schachtner, henceforth his devoted friend and admirer, would often lend him his own violin to practise on. The boy delighted in the smooth rich tone of this instrument, and called it descriptively " butter-fiddle." Its owner came in one day to find him amusing himself with his own little violin. Suddenly he stopped playing, and, after a moment's thought, he said solemnly : " I don't know what you have done with your butter-fiddle. If its tuning has not been changed since I last tried it, it is half a quarter of a tone flatter than mine here." Schachtner laughed incredulously; but he went and fetched his violin, and found that it was tuned exactly as Wolfgang had said.

An ear so sensitive as is revealed by the performance of this astonishing feat was obviously an instrument of extreme delicacy that would not bear rough handling. All through the years of his childhood Wolfgang had a strange horror of the sound of a trumpet. He could not bear to hear it played without other instruments, and even to see it handled in his presence filled him with as much alarm as if it had been a loaded pistol. Leopold was determined to remove this childish fear, a fear that he did not see was no less real because it was wholly unreasonable. Ignoring the boy's agonized entreaties he asked Schachtner to blow some trumpet blasts in his ear. At the first sound Wolfgang turned pale and sank to the ground in convulsions of terror, nor could anything restore his peace of mind till the hated instrument was removed out of his sight. It was certainly an ill-advised experiment, and, happily, the father was sensible enough to see that it must on no account be repeated, and that in the delicate business of training a genius a gentler method of discipline must be applied. From the first he held up before his children a high standard of work, and insisted on the duty of developing to the utmost the talents that God had given to them. He was always telling them that the exceptional richness of their endowment and the fact that every kind of musical exercise came more easily to them than to others were reasons not for less but for more sustained efforts towards self-improvement. The richer the prize that was within their reach, the more vigorous should be their striving to attain it.

The children's life in their Salzburg home must have been sufficiently strenuous, for, besides the various musical activities that were always on foot, Leopold was careful to see that the ordinary subjects of education were not neglected, and he made them write, every evening, a short account of all that they had learnt or done during the day. Wolfgang's first studies in arithmetic were pursued with such ardour that they threatened to supplant even music in his affections, and for a time the manipulation of figures was as fascinating to him as the picking out of thirds and sixths on the harpsichord. He also showed a decided aptitude for foreign languages, which later his father was constantly urging him to practise and develop when he took him on tour through the cities of Europe. When he grew older he was fond of exercising his linguistic skill on his sister, and, in many a joking letter to her, nonsense scraps of German, French, Italian, and Latin would be jumbled together in a single sentence.

But music, of course, was the dominating interest of his life, and when he was occupied with that he would allow no frivolity or jokes to distract him. Many years afterwards, his father, in one of the moral lectures that he was never tired of delivering, reminded him of the intense seriousness with which he applied himself to music in his childish days, and how when he was playing or composing the expression of his face was so grave that many who saw it prophesied his early death. Music was not only his favourite subject of study, it was the natural accompaniment of everything he did in work or play.

In the Mozart family life the mother played a quite inconspicuous part. She was an amiable, easy-going woman, with little force of character, and no intellectual or artistic distinction, content to remain all her life in the honourable obscurity of the typical *Hausfrau* and to resign all matters that lay outside that narrow sphere to the masterful hands of her husband. Wolfgang was always dutifully affectionate towards her, but there was no real community of feeling or interest between them, and when, at a later time, she undertook, single-handed, the charge of her son on a journey abroad, she showed a pathetic incapacity for the task, and her attempts to exercise maternal authority resulted only in friction and mutual misunderstanding.

Many great men through the ages have witnessed to the unrepayable debt they owed to a mother's guidance and sympathy; the case of Mozart was an exception to the common experience. For him the dominating influence was his father. His childish motto—" God first, and then papa "—became the rule of his life. The father's loving care that tended the opening bud of the boy's genius continued through all the years of its splendid blossoming. The discipline begun in the nursery and the schoolroom was exercised with hardly diminished force and insistence on the grown man, and Wolfgang, a child in spirit to the end, never entirely lost the habit of deferring to his father's counsel and of judging everything that he did or purposed by the touchstone of his father's approval. On the effect of this life-long tutelage the verdict of Schachtner, the old family friend, is probably just. Writing, after Mozart's death, to the sister who had asked him to tell her what he could remember of her brother's childhood, he said: " He was full of fire; his inclinations were easily swayed. I believe that had he been without the advantages of the good education which he received, he might have become a profligate scoundrel—he was so ready to yield to every attraction which offered."

CHAPTER III

Salzburg and the Seven Years' War—Mozart family visit
Vienna—social triumphs—Wolfgang at the palace—
proposes to Marie Antoinette—he falls ill—family
return home.

WOLFGANG MOZART was born in the first year of
the Seven Years' War, and while the efforts of the
combined Powers—Austria, France, Russia, and
Sweden—to destroy the power of Frederick the
Great were drenching Europe with blood, there
was growing up in a humble Salzburg home one
of the world's great masters of music. The tide of
battle surged to and fro through years of varying
fortune, and in the end the protagonists sank back,
exhausted, into an inconclusive peace. These
momentous events hardly ruffled the surface of life
in Salzburg. The place was well removed from
the sphere of military operations; its eyes were
directed rather towards Italy in the south than
towards Germany in the north. For centuries it
had been the seat of a great feudal archbishopric,
and it was thus too closely connected with the
Church to be a city of true German feeling.

Like his fellow-citizens Leopold Mozart looked
on at the clash of the contending armies with
impartial unconcern. His letters contain scarcely
an allusion to the struggle that was raging in
Europe, and throughout the war years he applied
himself to his official duties at the Archbishop's
court, and to the education of his two children, in

undisturbed seclusion. But other schemes were forming in his mind. While, as a pious Catholic, he desired that the marvellous musical gifts of his children, coming as they did from the hand of God, should be used to redound to His glory, he realized that they might serve the more mundane purpose of bringing considerable pecuniary profit to himself. The musical accomplishments of Wolfgang and Marianne, as soon as the state of Europe made it possible, must be displayed on a wider stage than that of Salzburg. So in the autumn of 1762, when peace was reasonably well assured though not actually signed, Leopold and his family set out for Vienna, and the little Wolfgang had his first sight of the city which was to be his home for the last ten years of his life, and where the ripest fruits of his genius were to be produced.

The boy was not long in turning his musical gifts to profitable account. When the family, on arrival in the town, were confronted with the demand for customs dues, he softened the official heart by showing him his clavier and playing him a minuet on his fiddle; " that," his father recorded triumphantly, " passed us through."

But the children's music passed them through more important barriers than those of the *douane*. Vienna received them with open arms. Reports of their charming manners and their astonishing precocity spread through the town, and parties given to hear them perform soon became the fashionable form of entertainment. Invitations to the houses of the great poured in on the Mozart family, and the nobles and grand ladies of Vienna, wearied with the anxiety and strain of the long war years, eagerly yielded themselves to the enjoyment of their new playthings.

The obscure Salzburg music-master suddenly

awoke to find himself an honoured guest in the mansions of a great European capital. He sent home exciting accounts of the family's social triumphs. " To-day," he wrote, " we were at the French Ambassador's, and to-morrow we shall go to Count Harrach's. We are everywhere fetched and sent back in the carriages of the nobility. We have agreed to be present from six to nine o'clock at a grand concert, in which all the greatest artists of Vienna will perform. Not to be too late, we are engaged four, five, even eight days in advance, as was the case with the Postmaster-General on Monday. On one occasion we were at a house from half-past two till near four o'clock; then Count Hardegg sent his carriage for us, which took us full gallop to the house of a lady, where we stayed till half-past five; afterwards we were with Count Kauniz till near nine." " Everywhere," he added, " the ladies are in love with my boy."

Soon there came the crowning excitement of an invitation to the Austrian Court. " At present," Leopold wrote, " I have not time to say more than that we had so gracious a reception from both their Majesties that my account of it might be taken for a fable. Wolfgang sprang into the lap of the Empress, took her round the neck, and kissed her very heartily. We were there from three to six o'clock, and the Emperor himself came into the ante-chamber to fetch me in to hear the child play on the violin. Yesterday the Empress sent us, through her private treasurer, who drove up in state before the door of our lodgings, two robes, one for the boy, the other for the girl. Wolfgang's dress is of a lily colour, of the finest cloth, with a waistcoat of the same, and the coat with double broad gold borders. It was made for the Archduke Maximilian. Marianne's dress is the court costume of an Archduchess. It is of white brocaded taffeta, with all sorts of ornaments."

The children in their smart Court dress, playing merry little pieces on harpsichord or violin, won all hearts, and they soon became established favourites at Schönbrunn. The Emperor Francis called Wolfgang the little magician, and would jokingly test his powers by making him play on the keys covered with a handkerchief.

Music was much cultivated at the Court, and most of the members of the Imperial family were sufficiently versed in the art to take a discriminating delight in the performances of their wonderful little guests. The great Maria Theresa herself, accomplished in all the graceful arts, found relief from the cares of State in dance and song, and her son Joseph, afterwards Emperor, had a fine bass voice and played the clavier and violin with more than ordinary skill. It was this prince who found himself exposed to the first strokes of the young Wolfgang's critical sword. He was playing a solo on the violin when from the ante-room where the Mozarts were waiting there came the cry, in a confident treble, "Ah! that was out of tune," and then, as he passed to another phrase, an encouraging "Bravo!" The boy, it was clear, was no obsequious courtier. Judgments on musical matters, bold and unqualified, came naturally to the lips of one who throughout his life was to be a rebel against authority, who, where music was concerned, would care neither for prince nor noble, and would be loyal only to the high artistic standard that he set up for himself.

One of the Mozarts' visits to the palace resulted, so the story goes, in an early offer of marriage to Marie Antoinette. The future Queen of France, then a little girl of seven, and her sister were leading Wolfgang across the polished floor of the royal boudoir to the Empress. The boy's foot slipped and he fell to the ground. One of his guides took no notice of the accident, but Marie Antoinette lifted him up and consolingly wiped away his tears. Prompt came the grateful response, " You are very kind, I will marry you." The Empress asked Wolfgand how he came to form such a resolution. " From gratitude," he replied; " she was so good to me, but her sister stood by and did nothing."

In the midst of all these diversions there came a sudden check. Wolfgäng fell ill of scarlet fever, and, though the attack was not serious, the family had perforce to pass several weeks in profitless seclusion. Many of the Mozarts' friends among the Viennese nobility sent to inquire after the boy's health, but Leopold was disappointed at receiving nothing more tangible than messages of sympathy. He was able, indeed, to save his purse by paying the doctor's bill with music instead of in hard cash, but the cutting off of the source of profit from his children's musical performances was a serious blow to his hopes. He decided that for the present it would be rash to tempt fortune further. Abitious schemes for the future were floating in his head, but their time was not yet ripe. So, as soon as Wolfgang's recovery was complete, the family took their leave of Vienna, and by the beginning of 1763 they were back in Salzburg.

CHAPTER IV

Leopold's grand tour—his abilities as showman—visit to
Paris—family at Versailles—Wolfgang and La Pompadour—Leopold criticizes French social manners—leaves
for England.

THE year 1763 saw the return of peace to a war-
weary Europe, and the field at last was clear for
Leopold Mozart to carry out the ambitious scheme
that had been revolving in his mind. His two
children were already accomplished musicians;
Marianne, at the age of twelve, played the clavier
with all the assurance of a mature virtuoso, and
the seven-year-old Wolfgang not only rivalled his
sister as a performer on clavier and violin, but had
given the first clear signs of that creative genius
which was to win for him immortality. The time
had come when they should display their powers
before the most distinguished and critical audiences
in the land. A grand European tour was planned :
Germany, France, England, Holland, were the
countries marked out for peaceful conquest, the
scenes of a triumphal progress which would bring
fame and fortune to the Mozart family.

On the 9th of June the party—father, mother,
and two children—set out from Salzburg, and it
was more than three years before they were to see
their home again. The expedition was a formid-
able undertaking which might well have daunted
the courage of an even more determined leader
than Leopold. Confronting him was the anxious

task of balancing the family budget, with the knowledge that the expenses of travel must be met out of the precarious proceeds of his children's concerts, and the uncertain favours of noble patrons. Certainly, also, he would need to exercise unremitting care in guarding the child musicians, on whose exploits the success of the tour depended, against the risks of fatigue and overstrain. Leopold faced the prospect boldly. He decided at the outset that the party should travel "*noblement*," as he put it, not only for the preservation of their health, but for the credit of the archiepiscopal court, and he was confident that in the musical talents of Marianne and Wolfgang there was a potential gold mine which would amply repay him for this unwonted extravagance.

For a time all went smoothly. In the Bavarian towns with which the party began their tour Wolfgang added the conquest of a new instrument— the organ—to his trophies. At Wasserburg his father took him up to the organ loft of the cathedral and explained to him the working of the pedals. The lesson had not proceeded far before the boy impatiently pushed away the stool and, standing upright on the pedal-board, began to improvise with complete ease and assurance. The church now became the chief point of attraction in each town that he visited, and wherever access to the organ could be had he would spend happy hours in exercising his newly-found powers. At Heidelberg he was allowed to give a miniature organ recital in the chief church of the town. Here his fame as a boy prodigy had preceded him, and a large crowd, including the dean and canons of the church, assembled to hear him play. For an hour he held them spellbound, and the dean, profoundly moved, at once ordered that his name should be inscribed on the organ " as an eternal remembrance."

Besides these organ triumphs, Wolfgang and his sister performed with brilliant success at concerts of clavier and violin music in each town they visited. Among their audience on one occasion was Goethe, then a boy of fourteen. Long afterwards he recalled how he had seen the little Mozart, with his powdered wig and his sword, playing the harpsichord in a Frankfort concert hall.

Wherever they went Leopold played the part of travelling showman with untiring energy and skill. The announcements of the concerts at which the children were to appear read almost like the advertisements of a provincial circus with acrobats and performing animals. Here is one of them :

" The little girl, who is in her twelfth year, will play the most difficult compositions of the greatest masters; the boy, who is not yet seven, will perform on the clavecin or harpsichord; he will also play a concerto for the violin, and will accompany symphonies on the clavier, the keyboard being covered with a cloth, with as much facility as if he could see the keys; he will instantly name all notes played at a distance, whether singly or in chords, on the clavier, or on any other instrument, bell, glass, or clock. He will finally, both on the harpsichord and the organ, improvise as long as may be desired and in any key."

The children, it will be seen, were frankly exhibited as prodigies, rather than as artists; nothing was omitted that might enhance the marvel of their performance, even to the understatement of Wolfgang's age, who at that time was not under seven but well on in his eighth year.

The father's belief in his children's exceptional powers was indeed amply justified, and wherever

they went their performances aroused unbounded
enthusiasm. But the financial return on all the
effort expended was disappointing. The German
nobility, for all the surface show of old-time
splendour in which they lived, were mostly
impoverished, and they preferred to express their
admiration for the children's music in pretty
presents than in cash payment. There were swords
and snuff-boxes for Wolfgang, lace and china
trinkets for Marianne—enough, as their father
said, to set up a shop but not to pay their travelling
expenses. Leopold's thrifty soul, with the ambitious
project of visits to Paris and London before him,
was clouded with doubt and apprehension. Even
an attractive proposal from Princess Amelia, sister
of Frederick the Great and a musical amateur of
distinction, who had taken a great fancy to the
Mozart children when she heard them play at Aix
la Chapelle, had to be critically received. She
offered to take them to display their powers at the
Berlin Court, but Leopold knocked the pretty
scheme on the head. "The Princess has no
money," he said; "if the kisses she bestows on
Master Wolfgang were each a louis d'or, we should
be well off; as it is, neither our hotel bill nor our
post-horses can be paid with kisses." Frederick
was a great lover of music and a flute-player of
almost professional attainments, but he had a
rooted disbelief in the musical capacity of his
countrymen, and he used to say that he would as
soon expect to receive pleasure from the neighing
of his horse as from a German singer. Such pre-
judice could hardly have survived an hour of
Wolfgang's playing, and it must have been a sore
disappointment to Leopold to be obliged to forgo
the opportunity of adding so illustrious a victim
to the tale of his son's conquests.

The Mozarts reached Paris by the middle of
November, and the anxieties which had been
weighing on Leopold's mind melted away in the
genial warmth of the welcome extended to them
on all sides. The Bavarian Ambassador, whose
wife was the daughter of an official in the Archbishop's court at Salzburg, gave them lodging and
generous entertainment; and they brought with
them letters of introduction to several of the leading figures in Parisian society. Among them was
one commending them to the notice of Friedrich
Melchior Grimm, which as a passport to social
advancement Leopold regarded, not without
reason, as worth all the others put together. Grimm,
the most French of all the Germans, had been
living in Paris for several years, and now held a
dominating position in the literary and artistic life
of the capital. Secretary to the Duke of Orleans,
intimate friend of Diderot, a fastidious and learned
connoisseur of the arts, literary correspondent with
half the sovereigns of Europe, he made it his
business to keep eyes and ears always open to
recognize the promise of any outstanding talent or
genius; and it needed but a few days' acquaintance
with the Mozart family to convince him that here
was a fitting object for his discriminating benevolence. Leopold wrote to his friends at Salzburg in
delighted anticipation of the triumphs that awaited
him in Paris under this powerful patronage, and
spoke enthusiastically of his new friend's kindliness
and condescension. It was very different from the
disagreeable picture of Grimm drawn in Rousseau's
Confessions, but Grimm's *liaison* with his friend's
mistress, Madame d'Epinay, had produced an
irreconcilable breach between the two men, and
Rousseau's pen was dipped in gall. Leopold's
estimate was simpler and probably a good deal

more veracious. "What cannot a man do," he exclaimed, "with sense and a kind heart? Grimm has been fifteen years in Paris, and knows how to make things fall out as he wishes."

Grimm quickly showed that this confidence in his power was not misplaced by procuring for the Mozarts an introduction to the Court of Versailles. Here the long reign of Madame de Pompadour was nearing its end, and Leopold gave an impression of her as she appeared to him in the last months of her life. "She must have been very beautiful," he wrote, "for she is still an elegant person. Her figure is imposing; she is large and plump, but well proportioned; her complexion is fair, with some likeness to Her Imperial Majesty about the eyes. She is proud, and has a remarkable mind. Her apartments looking on to the gardens at Versailles are like a paradise, and she has a magnificent hotel just built in the Faubourg St. Honoré. In the room where the harpsichord was, which was gilt and beautifully ornamented and painted, we observed her portrait and the king's, both of life size."

At the gates of this paradise Leopold and his family duly presented themselves, and were conducted with all proper ceremony into the presence of the uncrowned queen of France. The rooms set apart by the King for his mistress's use were of world-famous loveliness, harmonizing so perfectly with the gardens in which they stood that it was difficult to say which was the jewel and which the setting. The crown and climax of the whole was the Marquise's own boudoir; furnished and adorned by Louis at a fabulous cost, it was a shrine worthy of the goddess whose beauty the passage of forty years had scarcely dimmed. Here on the threshold the Mozart family stood bewildered at

3

the dazzling scene which met their eyes. La
Pompadour rose with a friendly gesture of greeting
to relieve their embarrassment; then she took the
little Wolfgang in her arms and stood him on a
table in front of her chair. It was a commanding
point of vantage, and from it the boy bent forward
to kiss his lady's cheek. But she pushed him gently
aside; he must learn that so rich a fruit could not
be thus lightly tasted. Wolfgang, remembering the
caresses freely lavished upon him by Maria Theresa
and her daughters, was puzzled and hurt at the
unexpected rebuff. "Who is this that does not
want to kiss me?" he cried; "Why, the Empress
kissed me!"

Amid all these excitements Leopold managed to
keep his critical eye wide open, and, in his letters
from Paris to friends at Salzburg, glowing descrip-
tions of the family triumphs were interspersed with
much comment on the poor quality of French
music and on the vices and follies of French society.

In the contest then raging in Paris between
French and Italian music he was in whole-hearted
agreement with his friend Grimm. "French
music," he wrote, "the whole of it put together, is
not worth a straw"; and he hoped it would not be
long before this spurious form of art would have
vanished altogether from the world. As for his
Wolfgang, he could play anything that was placed
before him, whether French or Italian, with equal
mastery, and Leopold looked forward to the time
when a Mozart would establish a new German
sovereignty in musical Europe before which both
the rival schools would lay their faded laurels.

The manners of French society were no better
than its music; "pomp and splendour," Leopold
wrote, "are still extravagantly admired and pursued by the French . . . the gentry are overwhelmed

with debts, no one is rich but the farmers and bankers, and their money is chiefly spent on Lucretias, who, however, do not stab themselves."

The consequences of the unnatural practice prevailing among the Parisians of abandoning their new-born children to the care of peasant nurses were described in unpleasant detail: "You will hardly find any place so abounding in miserable and mutilated objects. Scarcely have you been two minutes in a church, or walked through a couple of streets, when you are beset by some blind, lame, deformed, or half-putrefying beggar; or you see someone lying in the street whose hand when he was a child was devoured by a pig; or another who fell into the fire and had half his arm burnt off." Leopold reserved his final shaft for the flaunting fineries of the demimonde: "As for their religion, the miracles of the French female saints, I assure you, are not scarce; the greatest are performed by those who are neither maids, wives, nor widows, and are all worked by the living body. Suffice it to say that it costs some trouble here to discover who is the mistress of the house; everyone lives according to his or her fancy, and if there is not a special mercy of God, it will one day fare with the state of France as of old with the kingdom of Persia." With which solemn denunciation Leopold shook off the dust of Paris from his feet and set out with his family on a new enterprise on the other side of the English Channel.

CHAPTER V

THE Mozarts' life in Paris had been rich in exciting experiences. The town had rung with the praises of the two wonderful children, and the Court of Louis XV, long abandoned to a ceaseless round of coarse and frivolous pleasures, had taken Wolfgang and Marianne to their hearts and, listening night after night to their music, had felt a new and thrilling emotion which lifted them for a moment above themselves. But Leopold had found that the position of Court favourites and idols of the Parisian public entailed an expensive mode of living which made serious in-roads into the profits of the tour. The English, he believed, were richer and no less generous than the French, and a visit to a country well known for its readiness to give an appreciative welcome to foreign musicians would be a sure means of enabling him to retrieve the family fortunes. So the party started on the journey to London with high hopes. At Calais the children had their first sight of the sea, and there is a picturesque entry in Marianne's diary describing how the waves " run away and come back again." The Dover packet was small and overcrowded, and both parents and children were very seasick. The discomforts of the journey, however, were soon forgotten in the warmth of the welcome which awaited them in London. They found convenient lodgings at the house of a Mr. Williamson in Frith Street, Soho, and in little more than a fortnight after their arrival they received a summons to the Court of George III and Queen Charlotte. Two evenings of music-making were spent with the royal family, and Leopold, even with memories of the triumphs won at Schönbrunn and Versailles fresh in his mind, confessed that their reception at the Court of St. James' put all previous experiences into the shade. He spoke of the " indescribable condescension of both the exalted personages," and of their manners, so friendly and familiar, that it was impossible to believe they were the King and Queen of England. In this congenial atmosphere Wolfgang entertained the company with a wonderful display of versatility. He played off at sight a number of pieces by Handel and others which the King placed before him to test his powers; then, running from the harpsichord to the organ, he performed on that instrument with even greater mastery; a little later in the evening he was again at the harpsichord, accompanying the Queen in a song, and playing the clavier part of a flute sonata. As he finished, the bass part of a Handel air lying on the desk caught his eye, and on this he improvised a charming melody that would have rejoiced the old master's heart. It was the forerunner of the delicious counterpoint with which in later years he was to adorn the score of *Messiah*.

Among the company who had been listening to the boy's playing was John Christian Bach, youngest son of the great Sebastian, who had followed Handel as music-master to the royal family, and who was destined, like him, to experience the fickleness of the fashionable London world. Just now his star was in the ascendant. His facile talent gained for him an eminence far exceeding that of his mighty father, and, when one of his pretty operas was given at the King's Theatre, the doors were besieged with eager crowds who had never even heard of the *B Minor Mass* or the *St. Matthew Passion*. In later years his popularity waned before the brightness of new favourites. Neglect and penury succeeded to affluence, and he died leaving a legacy to his widow of some £4,000 less than nothing.

Bach, as he listened to Wolfgang, realized that he was in the presence of genius. He went up to the harpsichord, took the boy on his knee, and together they went through a sonata, playing alternate bars with all the precision of a pair of accomplished jugglers tossing balls to each other. Then he began a fugue and, after statement of subject and counter-subject, stopped for a moment; Wolfgang promptly took up the running and carried the piece to a perfectly appropriate conclusion. This delightful duet was the beginning of a lasting friendship between the two composers. They were destined to meet but seldom in after years, but Mozart became a devoted admirer of Bach's music, and his mature works show distinct signs of its influence on his style.

With the brilliant success of the evening at the palace, the Mozarts' life in London opened under the fairest auspices. A few days afterwards, on a fine May morning, they were taking the air in St. James' Park. Down the Mall came the royal carriage with an escort of Life Guards—on glossy black horses—their plumed helmets glittering in the spring sunshine. It was a brave sight, and Wolf-

gang and Marianne, with excited cries, seized
their parents' arms and rushed forward to secure
a closer view. They were well rewarded. The
King instantly recognized them, though they had
exchanged the smart dresses they had worn at the
palace for more homely garb; he threw open the
carriage window and waved his hand at the
children with a friendly smile of greeting. A second
invitation to the palace quickly followed, and there
the Mozarts gave another evening of lovely music,
more intimate and domestic than the first, the
King with his brother and the Queen with her
brother being the only audience.

But Leopold had not brought his family to
England merely to bask in the sunshine of royal
favour. It was time to proceed to the more serious
business of turning the exploits of his two infant
prodigies into gold. So he boldly announced a
grand public concert to take place on the 5th of
June—a carefully chosen date, as the King's birthday festivities of the previous day might be
expected to bring a large concourse to the town.
A professional orchestra was engaged at what
seemed to Leopold an outrageously expensive cost,
and the solo performers on harpsichord and violin
were to be Marianne and Wolfgang Mozart.
Leopold, with the showman's instinct for drafting
advertisements, allured the London public by
promising that they should see and hear "the
greatest wonder of which Europe or the world can
boast." The bait attracted more fish into the net
than he had ever dared to hope; the hall was filled
with a fashionable and enthusiastic crowd, and, as
most of the orchestral players generously refused
to take a fee, the concert resulted in a clear profit
of no less than one hundred guineas.

Leopold wrote home a glowing account of this

concert and of the *furore* created by the children's playing. "My girl," he said, "is now esteemed the first female performer in Europe, though only twelve years old, and the high and mighty Wolfgang, though only eight, possesses the acquirements of a man of forty."

A request for the boy to be allowed to appear in the cause of charity at an entertainment at Ranelagh was the natural English sequel to this public triumph. The thrifty Leopold was not altogether enamoured of the idea, but, consoling himself with the thought that this was the way to gain the love of the English, he gave his consent, and Wolfgang played an organ concerto on this occasion which, his father recorded, "astonished and delighted the greatest connoisseurs in England."

The family's prosperous career in London was brought to a stop by the sudden illness of their head. Leopold fell seriously ill of quinsy, and for some days his life was despaired of. While he lay in the throes of the struggle with death, all instruments of music which had been sounding ceaselessly in the little house were hushed. Wolfgang, banished for the time from his beloved harpsichord and violin, quietly betook himself to the writing-desk and began work on his first symphony. By his side sat Marianne, copying out in a fair hand her brother's rough sketches. He had always been fascinated by the characteristic colour of the different wind instruments. The trumpet, we remember, had filled his childish soul with speechless terror, the oboe pierced it with a strange poignancy; and now in England he had learnt to love the horn, the soft human tones of which could in a moment transport him into the fairyland of his dreams. "Remind me," he said to his sister

as he bent over the score, " remind me to give
something really good to the horn." The prompt-
ing was hardly necessary, for from his earliest
years he seemed to know by instinct what was the
most telling and characteristic contribution that
each instrument could make to the *ensemble* of
concerto or symphony. Through the weeks of en-
forced silence the young composer worked indus-
triously; his father gradually won his way back to
health and vigour, and Wolfgang was able to
celebrate the happy issue by presenting him with
the manuscript of his Symphony No. 1 in E flat
major.

With Leopold now convalescent, the family
removed from Soho to the rural solitudes of
Chelsea, and found lodgings in the house of a
Mr. Randall in Five Field Row. Leopold's thank-
offering for his recovery took a rather unusual
form. Not only did he order twenty-two masses to
be said for his soul's welfare, but he undertook in
his leisure time the pious task of converting a
certain violoncello player, Sipruntini, the son of a
Dutch Jew, to the Christian faith.

Through the summer months music continued
to flow from Wolfgang's pen. Three more symphonies were completed, small in scale but with
all the structural finish of a born master of form;
and when, in the autumn, the family were again
summoned to Court to celebrate the fourth anni-
versary of the King's accession, Leopold was able,
in gratitude for the royal favour, to print a set of
six of his son's violin sonatas and to dedicate them
to Queen Charlotte, from Her Majesty's " trés
humble et trés obéissant petit serviteur." But to
Wolfgang an even more important event was the
opening of the Italian Opera House in November.
Night after night he would sit with his father in

the gallery, listening to the great stars of the operatic stage, while the delighted London public greeted each favourite aria with tumultuous plaudits. Here was sown the seed that was to grow into the lovely flowers of *Figaro* and *Don Giovanni*. With all his easy mastery of every branch of the musical art, opera was the really dominant passion of his life, and now the first taste of it was intoxicating. He could think of nothing else. " His head," wrote Leopold, " is at present full of an opera which he wishes to have performed by his Salzburg friends, and I am often obliged to reckon up the young people who are to compose his orchestra." The king of the London opera stage at that time was the Florentine tenor, Giovanni Manzuoli, and Wolfgang could not rest till his father obtained an introduction to the great man. This was duly achieved; Manzuoli took a great fancy to the boy and completely won his heart by volunteering to give him singing lessons. The little treble voice developed remarkably under the master's guidance, and Grimm, who, a year later, heard him in Paris, remarked how delighted he was at the exquisite taste and expressiveness of his singing.

The genuineness of the possession of such astonishing musical powers by a boy of eight was not allowed to pass entirely without challenge. The Hon. Daines Barrington's suspicions were aroused. This gentleman, after an undistinguished career as a Welsh judge, was now settled in London, occupying himself with the more congenial work of philosophical and antiquarian research. He had an insatiable thirst for inquiring into curious phenomena of all kinds, and the young Mozart's precocious musical development seemed eminently a subject which called for his careful

investigation. So he introduced himself to Leopold, and with his leave applied the most exacting
tests that he could devise to the boy's musical skill.
He brought with him the manuscript score of a
vocal duet, with accompaniment of two violins and
a bass, composed by an English amateur, to some
words in an opera of Metastasio's, and required
Wolfgang to sing the upper part at sight while
playing the string accompaniment on the harpsichord. This task was accomplished with the utmost ease: "his voice," Mr. Barrington tells us,
"in the tone of it was thin and infantine, but
nothing could exceed the masterly manner in
which he sung." Leopold took the lower part in
the duet with a good deal less than his son's
accuracy, and now and again the boy would look
up reproachfully at his father standing behind him
and point out the mistakes that he was making.
Mr. Barrington then said he would like to hear an
extempore love-song such as Manzuoli might
choose in an opera. The mention of the great
singer's name acted like magic. The boy looked
back from his seat at the harpsichord "with much
archness" and, after a few bars of jargon recitative, delivered himself of an impassioned operatic
aria on the single word *Affetto*. "If this extem-
porary composition was not amazingly capital,"
said Mr. Barrington, "yet it was really above
mediocrity, and shewed most extraordinary readiness of invention." He next asked him to compose
a "Song of Rage, such as might be proper for
the opera stage." Again the arch look back from
the harpsichord seat, again the introductory jargon
recitative, and then an aria of anger and scorn
inspired by the word *Perfido,* as dramatically
appropriate as the love-song had been. "In the
middle of it," said Mr. Barrington, "he had

worked himself up to such a pitch that he beat his harpsichord like a person possessed, rising sometimes in his chair." Yet in the intervals between these feats of genius he was the ordinary human boy again. If a favourite cat came in while he was playing, he would jump down from the stool and fondle it; " he would also sometimes run about the room with a stick between his legs by way of horse."

The Hon. Daines Barrington was astonished, but still not wholly convinced. All his musical friends in London told him it was impossible that a child of such tender years could surpass the greatest masters in their own science. Leopold, they hinted, was imposing on him in regard to his son's age. He must see the birth certificate. So he applied to the Bavarian envoy, and through him procured an extract from the Salzburg register for the year 1756, which finally set his doubts at rest.

Mr. Barrington gave a vivid description of his visit to the Mozarts in a paper which he wrote for the Royal Society. The gentle irony of its opening sentence is engaging : " If I was to send you a well-attested account of a boy who measured seven feet in height when he was not more than eight years of age, it might be considered as not undeserving the notice of the Royal Society. The instance which I now desire you will communicate to that learned body, of as early an exertion of most extraordinary musical talents, seems perhaps equally to claim their attention."

The author included the paper in a volume of *Miscellanies* in which he gathered up the varied fruits of his curious investigations. Here, side by side with disquisitions " On the Possibility of reaching the North Pole "; " Whether the Turkey was known before the Discovery of America ";

" On the Torpidity of the Swallow Tribe when they disappear "; " On the Deluge in the Time of Noah," there appeared " An Account of Mozart, a very remarkable young Musician."

Meanwhile, Leopold continued to provide the London public with opportunities of hearing the child prodigies. But the charm of novelty had worn off, and, while the expenses of public concerts remained as high as ever, the takings at the doors began to show a serious falling off. Even flaming announcements of the appearance of the " Wonder of Nature," and hints that this might be the last occasion on which he could be heard in London, failed to attract. Leopold then tried the plan of inviting the public to come and test the Wonder's powers at private séances daily from twelve to two o'clock, first in their own lodging and then in a hired room in a tavern; the children, he promised, would perform the feat that had fascinated European royalties of playing a duet on the clavier with the keyboard covered. It was all of no avail, and Leopold gave vent to his disappointment and chagrin in a petulant outburst on the degradation of English manners. " I am determined," he wrote, " not to bring up my children in so dangerous a place as London, where the people for the most part have no religion, and there are scarcely any but bad examples before one's eyes." It was a little curious that the pagan tendencies of Londoners should not have been discovered till their attendance at concerts of the Mozart children had begun to fall off. But, in any case, Leopold had now a double reason for bringing his English visit to an end, and his decision was quickly taken. The last weeks of the Mozarts' stay in London were largely occupied with sight-seeing, and a long visit to the British Museum, which had been only recently opened, was marked by an appreciative entry in Marianne's diary and a description of the curiosities of natural history which particularly took her fancy. Wolfgang suggested to his father that they ought to make a present to the Museum as a memento of the visit. So he composed a little sacred motet, "God is our Refuge," and this manuscript, together with copies of his printed sonatas, was duly added to the treasures of the national collection. Leopold received an official letter from the secretary saying that "he was ordered by the standing committee of the trustees to signify that they had received the present of the musical performances of your very ingenious son and to return their thanks for the same."

Leopold's leave of absence from the Archbishop's service at Salzburg had now long expired, but a pressing invitation from the Prince of Orange at the Hague, conveyed through the Dutch Ambassador in London, induced him to postpone his return home for a few months more. The visit to Holland was clouded by the serious illness of both the children. Marianne lay for a whole week in a state of delirium, hovering between life and death; an urgent message was sent to Salzburg asking for masses to be said for her soul and a priest was summoned to the bedside to administer the last offices of the Church. Leopold describes how he and his wife discoursed to her, in the intervals of consciousness, on the vanity of the world she was about to leave and on the blessedness of an early death, while Wolfgang sat quietly composing in the next room. The Prince of Orange sent gracious messages of sympathy to the stricken home, and his sister, the Princess von Weilburg, ordered her favourite physician to give his skilled advice on the treatment of the illness. With the aid of these various agencies, Marianne gradually recovered; but anxiety on her account had scarcely passed before her brother also was seized with a dangerous fever, which reduced him to a state of great bodily weakness but was powerless to quell his brave little spirit. Day after day, as he lay flushed and restless on his sick-bed, he would ask for pen and paper and a board to be laid across his knees, so that he might write down the musical ideas that were surging in his brain. Slowly he fought his way back to health; and, with the coming of spring, Leopold, with both his children strong and well again, was able to resume his travels. Amsterdam was the next halt, but here the Mozarts' visit threatened to be as musically unfruitful as the months they had spent at The Hague. It was Lent, and, by the Lutheran rule, all public entertainments were strictly forbidden. But the chance of hearing two infant prodigies was too good to be missed, and the Dutch Church authorities devised an ingenious escape from the *impasse*. The exhibition of the marvellous gifts of these children, they argued, would redound to the honour and glory of God, and performances with this noble object would surely be no desecration of the penitential season. So the ban was removed and two concerts were given, at which all the instrumental pieces were of Wolfgang's composition. Leopold, as a strict Catholic, had no love for the Lutherans, but their liberal gesture on this occasion softened his heart, and, with the substantial proceeds of the concerts in his pocket, he acclaimed their action as both wise and pious.

For the rest of the journey little serious musical enterprise was attempted. There was a second visit of a few days to Paris, then a holiday excursion into Switzerland, and at last the travellers turned their steps homewards. Marianne described in her diary how her brother, in the rare intervals when his mind was not occupied with music, found an outlet for his creative fancy. He would imagine himself the king of a fair and fruitful country, where his subjects were all good and happy children. The family servant who was travelling with them would be pressed into the service and made to draw a map of this Utopia, while the young monarch dictated to him the names of its towns and villages.

The three years of travel, with its mingled triumphs and disappointments, its joys and anxieties, had been, on the whole, a happy and profitable time, and as it drew to an end Leopold looked forward to the future with some misgiving. What sort of reception would they get on their return to Salzburg, he wondered? Would the conditions of life at home make possible the free and full development of his children's genius, on which, he was well aware, the whole fabric of his existence depended? " Perhaps," he concluded, " we shall be only too glad to take our knapsacks on our backs and be off again. At any rate, I offer my children to my country. If it will have none of them, that is not my fault, and will be my country's loss."

CHAPTER VI

Return to Salzburg—Wolfgang's oratorio—Vienna again—
   La Finta Semplice—performance at Salzburg—Wolfgang appointed Konzertmeister.

AFTER three years of wandering, rich in exciting
experiences and, to a modest degree, in pecuniary
profit, Leopold and his family took up again their
life of peaceful seclusion in Salzburg. The Archbishop accepted with a good grace his Kapellmeister's excuses for the prolonged absence,
listened attentively to the account of his travels,
and showed a lively interest in the little boy whose
musical exploits had astonished three European
Courts. But when Leopold brought out some of
the compositions that Wolfgang had written during
the tour, the Archbishop was frankly incredulous,
and he determined to test their genuineness by a
method of his own devising. He asked that the
boy might be shut up in the house for a week,
with pen and ink and music paper, without seeing
anyone; during this time he was to compose a
sacred oratorio on a libretto provided by the Archbishop himself. The worthy Sigismund was no
poet, and his pious doggerel on the spiritual
adventures of A Lukewarm Christian, the hero of
the drama, cannot have done much to cheer or
inspire the long days of imprisonment. But Wolfgang was nothing daunted, and by the end of the
week he had completed a score 208 pages long,
conforming faithfully to the recognized Italian

4   49

model, and here and there, in a passage of accompanied recitative, showing a real power of dramatic characterization. The little work was publicly performed in the Lent of 1767, and the Archbishop was among the audience who applauded the leading Salzburg tenor for the vigour he infused into the arias of A Lukewarm Christian.

Meantime, Leopold pursued his son's musical education with redoubled zeal. The boy, he was convinced, was a genius, and for that very reason he needed the strictest training in the fundamentals of his art that could be given. An exercise book preserved in the Salzburg Mozarteum, with the student's essays in harmony and counterpoint, all neatly corrected and annotated by the master, shows the conscientious thoroughness with which Leopold discharged his task. Wolfgang for his part was a lively and responsive pupil, and even in the dry pages of formal exercise his innate love of dramatization would break through. Sometimes he would think of the parts in a harmony lesson as noblemen of different rank. The alto was *il Signore,* the tenor *il Marchese,* the bass *il Duca,* and he imagined how the three characters might join in a pretty terzetto as the finale of an opera.

These strenuous studies were broken into by a request from the Salzburg University that Wolfgang should write the incidental music to the Latin play performed by the students at the end of each scholastic year. The piece chosen for 1767 was *Apollo et Hyacinthus,* and, as the old story was treated in the manner of an Italian opera, Wolfgang found the task entirely congenial. The Latin text was something of an obstacle to free musical expression, but the scholarly Leopold was at hand to help him with this, and by the time he had finished the setting he had picked up a considerable smattering of the language, an accomplishment which he was never tired of showing off in letters to his family and friends. The play was duly presented in the theatre of the university, and an impressive description of the composer appeared on the programme : " *Auctor operis musici nobilis dominus Wolfgangus Mozart, undecennis, filius nobilis ac strenui domini Leopoldi Mozart, Capellae Magistri.*"

Life, indeed, in Salzburg was active and interesting enough, but a *Wanderlust* had taken hold of Leopold and he was itching to be off again on fresh adventures. News of the approaching marriage of the Princess Josepha with King Ferdinand of Naples turned his thoughts in the direction of Vienna. As a loyal subject of the Emperor he would naturally wish to be present at so important a ceremony, and there would also be an opportunity of displaying to the Viennese public the progress of his son's genius. But misfortune dogged the travellers' footsteps. An epidemic of small-pox broke out in Vienna and carried off the Princess on the eve of her wedding. Leopold fled with his family to Olmütz, but there both the children sickened of the disease. It was now that a good Samaritan in the person of Count Podstatsky, who was Canon of Salzburg as well as Dean of Olmütz, came to the rescue. Regardless of the risk of infection, he took the whole family into his house, and provided for the sick children all the skilled medical attention that he could command. Leopold commemorated this heroic act in glowing terms. " I cannot tell you," he wrote to a Salzburg friend, " with what kindness and goodness we were treated; who else would have received a family under such circumstances, and that from an impulse of pure humanity? This good deed shall redound to the honour of the Count in the biography of our little one which I intend to publish some day." The biography was never written, but the good Count's deed in helping to save a precious life will assuredly not be forgotten. Marianne quickly recovered, but Wolfgang's attack was so severe that he lay blind for nine days, and for several weeks afterwards the utmost care had to be taken of his eyes. It was an anxious time for Leopold and his wife, but their host's unvarying kindness and consideration greatly lightened the strain. He allowed none of the expenses of the illness to fall on them, and the doctor, under whose care the children won their way back to health, would accept no return for his services but the present of an aria that Wolfgang composed for his little daughter.

At Vienna, whither the family returned early in 1768, difficulties soon thickened about their path, though the visit opened promisingly enough with a renewed invitation to the Court. Here there had been many changes since they were there six years before. The Emperor Francis had died suddenly, his son Joseph was reigning in his stead, and the widowed Maria Theresa, her spirit broken by the shock, had retired into a gloomy seclusion, and would spend long hours in prayer in her husband's vault, preparing for her own end. News of the Mozarts' arrival aroused happy memories. She had not forgotten the charms of the little boy who had jumped on to her lap, thrown his arms round her neck, and told her why it was that he intended to marry her daughter Marie Antoinette; and, as soon as she heard that the Salzburg family were in Vienna again, she summoned them to her side. Leopold described how the Empress, herself only recently recovered from an attack of small-pox, asked his wife with motherly solicitude about every detail of the children's illness, now and then affectionately patting her cheek or pressing her hands; while the Emperor talked with Wolfgang and his father upon music and other matters, and paid compliments to Marianne that brought many a blush to her face.

The Mozarts' life in Vienna, however, which opened so brightly, soon became overclouded. Wolfgang, though in years still a mere boy, was not far short of artistic maturity, and the musicians of the capital who had been quite ready to applaud the precocious exploits of a child of six began to cast envious and malicious eyes on one whose rising star threatened soon to outshine them all. Their plan of campaign was simple enough. It was to avoid all contact with the Mozart family, and to refuse every opportunity of testing Wolfgang's musical powers; then, in reply to questioners, they could say that it was scientifically impossible for a boy not yet in his teens to compose concertos and symphonies, and that the stories of his improvising fugues and playing difficult sonatas at sight were obviously mere quackery and imposture. This professional boycott had its effect on public opinion, and the few concerts that Leopold was able to arrange were poorly attended. Moreover, the prevalent dread of small-pox infection among the Viennese nobility closed the doors of many erstwhile hospitable houses against the children so long as any traces of the disease remained on their faces. The situation was serious; but a timely order from the Emperor that Wolfgang should compose an Italian opera and conduct a performance of it himself from his seat at the harpsichord promised a way of retrieving it. Here, thought Leopold, was an opportunity for the bold stroke that would establish once for all his son's reputation and silence the envious voices of the hostile cabal. The libretto of an *opera buffa—La Finta Semplice*—was produced by the " Theatrical Poet," Coltellini; a contract was concluded with Affligio, the manager of the opera-house, for the production of the work, with a fee of a hundred ducats for the composer; and Wolfgang set to work on the music of his first opera. He wrote with feverish speed and energy, and in a few weeks the whole score of twenty-five numbers was completed. Meanwhile, the hostile forces in Vienna began to be busy, and every conceivable device was employed to delay and ultimately wreck the production of the work. " The whole hell of music," wrote Leopold, " has bestirred itself to prevent the talent of a child from being known." Affligio was a swindling adventurer who ended his days in prison for forgery. He had not the smallest feeling for art or music, but he saw in the performance of an opera by a boy of twelve the possibility of bringing off a sensational *coup* which would fill his pockets. The singers encouraged him to make the venture by enthusiastic praise of Wolfgang's arias, but after the first rehearsal, which was deliberately mismanaged in order to make the music sound confused and ineffective, Affligio's resolution began to weaken. The music was good enough, he told Leopold, but a little too high in places; several alterations were necessary, and these must be talked over with the singers : meanwhile, he would put two other operas in rehearsal in case *La Finta Semplice* should ultimately be found unsuitable. Weeks of exasperating inaction followed; the expenses of a prolonged stay in Vienna reduced Leopold's funds to a low ebb, and neither the boy's opera nor the promised one hundred ducats for its composer showed any signs of appearing. Public opinion, under the influence of malicious rumours, became steadily more hostile. The opera, it was said, was the work not of Wolfgang but of his father; the orchestra could not of course be expected to play under the leadership of a mere boy; and the singers, who had acclaimed the music as a masterpiece when they first saw it, had now discovered that it was undramatic and for that reason could not be performed by them. Affligio met Leopold's repeated complaints with fair words and promises, but at last he threw off the mask and boldly announced that he could not produce *La Finta Semplice* at all: if Leopold insisted on the contract being honoured, it would do him no good, for he would take good care that the opera should be made to sound ridiculous and hissed off the stage.

It was a bitter blow for Leopold, and on the top of it there came news from Salzburg that his salary at the Archbishop's court had been suspended and would not be resumed until he returned home. He wrote at once to his master, with the adroit plea that the saving of his son's honour concerned the Archbishop as much as himself: " His highness does not retain cheats, mountebanks, and liars in his service and give them his gracious permission to travel into foreign parts, like conjurers throwing dust into people's eyes; no, they are respectable men who travel for the credit of their prince and fatherland, to tell the world what a miracle it has pleased God to work in Salzburg." Leopold could not put off the rôle of travelling showman with his boy as a performing animal. What really troubled him about the failure of *La Finta Semplice* in Vienna was the fear that it would make it necessary to postpone his cherished project of a grand tour in Italy until Wolfgang was of an age and growth that would diminish the wonder of his performances. In the end, however, matters did not turn out so badly as he had anticipated. Shaking the dust of faithless Vienna from their feet the Mozarts made their way home to Salzburg. Here the Archbishop welcomed them with unusual cordiality; as a compensation for all their disappointments he arranged a performance of Wolfgang's new opera by his own private company, and honoured the little composer by appointing him Konzertmeister to the court.

CHAPTER VII

Tour in Italy—Padre Martini—Wolfgang's exploit in Sistine Chapel—*Mitridate, Ascanio in Alba, Lucio Silla,* written for Milan theatre.

ITALY ruled the musical world of the eighteenth century with unchallenged authority, and a visit to that country for the study of her artistic methods and practice was an essential element in the training of musicians of every nationality. All through Mozart's youth Italian music held undisputed sway in the churches and theatres of Germany. Even men of strong original power like Handel and Gluck had taken their first steps under Italian tutelage. The great independent school of German music was still but a dream of the future, and Wolfgang Mozart, who was destined to be one of its founders, was given, in the natural course, an important part of his training in Italy, and based his early efforts at composition on Italian methods.

The Mozarts set out for Italy in the last days of 1769, and the fifteen months of their tour was a time of unsullied enjoyment for both father and son. Wolfgang was in the highest spirits, and he recounted his experiences to his sister at Salzburg in a series of delightful letters full of boyish jokes and chaff, written, often, in a nonsense jumble of all the languages that he could think of, with shrewd comments on the virtues and vices of the singers and dancers in the opera of each town he visited. Music at this time permeated the very air

57

of Italy. The monasteries and religious houses were
as much occupied with counterpoint as with
theology; church choirs vied with one another in
the performance of an ornate liturgy and the singing of elaborate masses and motets; there was
scarcely a town in the country which could not
boast of an opera-house and a company of accomplished singers; and it was quite common, as Dr.
Burney records, to see eminent performers carrying
their own instruments through the streets with as
much pride as a soldier does his sword or musket.
To this congenial atmosphere the whole nature,
physical and artistic, of the young Mozart responded eagerly. It was the happy springtime of
his life. His father described with delight his
plump and sturdy appearance, and how the fresh
air in travelling and the open fires of Italian houses
gave a healthy brown tint to his complexion.
" But," he added proudly, " he will never injure
himself by eating or drinking. He will not touch
anything which he thinks unwholesome, and eats
many days little or nothing."

The Mozarts' concert tour through the chief
Italian towns—Mantua, Milan, Bologna, Florence,
Rome, Naples—was a continuous triumph, though
there was the usual grumble from Leopold that
their receipts consisted " chiefly in admiration and
bravos," and their financial position might have
become difficult had they not been helped from
time to time by the hospitality of the monasteries.
At Naples they stayed for a few days with their
London acquaintance, the British Ambassador, Sir
William Hamilton, and his wife, the predecessor
of Nelson's Emma. " Lady Hamilton," wrote
Leopold, " is a very agreeable person, who per-
forms on the clavier with unusual expression. She
was much alarmed at having to play before Wolf-

gang." Perhaps she shared the superstitious feelings
of the Neapolitans, who at one of Wolfgang's concerts became greatly excited at his performance,
and insisted that the nimbleness of his left hand
technique was due to the magical properties of a
ring he was wearing. The boy, when he realized
what the commotion in the audience was about,
at once took off the ring, and provoked a redoubled outburst of applause by continuing to play
no less brilliantly without it.

Such successes with a susceptible Italian public
were easily won, but there were sterner tests to be
faced. Among the friends that the Mozarts made
in Italy was Padre Martini, most learned of con-
trapuntists, who was spending a studious old age
with the famous singer, Farinelli, in a villa near
Bologna. Wolfgang gave a lively account of his
visit there, his delight in Farinelli's collection of
musical instruments, each named after a great
Italian painter, and how he played on each of
them in turn; and then how Martini gave him a
theme on which he was to extemporize a fugue,
and how, confronted with this task, he felt like a
general who sees the whole of the enemy's forces
before him and is resolved to strike a decisive
blow. " My heart beat fast of course," he said,
" not from fear, but from impatience to begin the
battle." The ordeal was successfully passed, and
the two old men rewarded the victorious little
general with affectionate embraces.

Wolfgang met Martini again on the occasion of
his election to the Philharmonic Academy of
Bologna. As a trial of his skill in composition, he
was locked into a room by himself for three hours,
and given an " Antiphona " to be set in four parts.
Half an hour had scarcely passed before an
insistent knocking on the door announced that the

task was already done. Martini and his fellow
judges went into the room, and there stood Wolfgang with the manuscript of the finished exercise
in his hand. It did not take them long to decide
that the boy's part-writing was fully up to the
required standard, and by a unanimous vote they
recommended his admission to membership of the
Academy. Wolfgang always retained a deep
respect and affection for the old Padre : in later
years he would often consult him on points of
style and method in the composition of Church
music, and submit his essays in that branch of the
art to his expert judgment. Leopold also, at certain critical moments in the family fortunes, tried
to induce Martini to use his good offices on his
son's behalf, but his efforts never, apparently, drew
from the old man anything more valuable than a
kindly letter of sympathy and encouragement.

It was on the visit to Rome in the spring of 1770
that Wolfgang performed the most famous of his
feats of musical precocity. The travellers arrived
in the city in Holy Week, and on Maundy Thurs-
day they were present at the ceremonial Washing
of the Feet by the Pope, and heard the singing of
Allegri's *Miserere* at Tenebrae in the Sistine
Chapel. The *Miserere* was a precious treasure of
the Vatican, guarded with the utmost care; the
choristers who performed it every year were forbidden, on pain of excommunication, to take any
parts out of the chapel or to make copies of it.
But these stern restrictions had no terrors for
Wolfgang. He came away from the Sistine Chapel
with the music of the Tenebrae written, not on
paper, but on the tablets of his brain, and before
he went to bed that night he had produced a
complete copy of the *Miserere*. The day following,
Good Friday, there was a second performance of

the psalm. Wolfgang stole into the chapel with his manuscript concealed in his hat, and secretly noted one or two mistakes he had made in his first copy. Dr. Burney tells how, many years afterwards, he had an opportunity of comparing Wolfgang's corrected copy with the original, and found there was not a note wrong.

Leopold's letter to his wife and daugher describing Wolfgang's exploit had a rather disturbing effect on the Salzburg home, but he calmed their fears by assuring them that the Roman authorities were so much delighted with the young culprit that they had forgotten to call upon the Pope to excommunicate him. "You must not fail," he added, "to show this letter to everyone, and above all you must let His Grace the Archbishop know."

Meanwhile a commission to compose an opera for Christmas at Milan summoned Wolfgang to more serious work. A libretto on the subject of "Mitridate, Re di Ponto," was supplied by a Turin poet, a company of singers was selected for the principal parts, and the young composer was soon absorbed in the task of fitting arias to their individual voices and styles, which he said he liked to do as neatly as a tailor would fit them with coats. Once he had set to work on music, his whole nature seemed to change; the boisterous jokes and chaff were all put aside, and he became so grave that his father begged his Salzburg friends to help to cheer him up by putting a little merriment into their letters. His power of concentration was extraordinary, and much of *Mitridate* was composed under conditions which to an ordinary mortal would have been intolerably disturbing. "Above us," he wrote to his sister, "is a violinist, beneath us is another, next us is a singing master who gives lessons, and in the room opposite is an oboe-player. That is jolly for composing. It gives one plenty of ideas."

The performance of *Mitridate* at the Milan theatre was a triumphant success, and the voices of envious critics, who had predicted the impossibility of a young German boy producing an Italian opera, were drowned in the torrent of delighted applause that greeted the composer. The opera was given the unusual honour of performance for twenty consecutive nights, and the manager at once made a contract with Wolfgang to write another for the season of 1773.

The Mozarts now turned their steps homewards, stopping on their way for a few days of gay life at Venice. Here, as Leopold recorded, they were lavishly entertained by many a nobleman of the highest rank, who would often, after the night's festivity, insist on taking them back to their lodgings in his own gondola. He was a little uneasy, however, at the costliness of the fancy dress that they had to wear for these occasions. " Here am I," he said, as he looked at himself in the glass, " going to play the fool in my old age " (he was not much more than fifty at the time). " My comfort in the midst of such silly expenses is that the things can be used afterwards for linings or footcloths."

On their arrival at Salzburg in March 1771 they found awaiting them a commission to Wolfgang from the Empress Maria Theresa to compose a dramatic serenata for the marriage of the Archduke Ferdinand at Milan in the autumn. Old Hasse, who in earlier days had entered the lists as the rival of Handel, was to write an opera for the same occasion, and youth and age were to meet in friendly rivalry. In August, the Mozarts were

back in Milan; Wolfgang set to work on his serenata—*Ascanio in Alba*—and in two months it was
ready for performance. Leopold summed up the
situation by saying that his son's work had knocked
Hasse's opera on the head, and the old composer
was foremost in acclaiming his young rival's
triumph. "This boy," he prophesied, "will throw
us all into the shade."

The Mozarts paid one more visit to Italy, for
Wolfgang was under contract to write an opera
for the carnival at Milan in 1773. He applied
himself to the work with his usual concentrated
ardour; he wrote to his sister that he was so much
absorbed that he was in danger of sending her an
entire aria instead of a letter. The production of
Lucio Silla was greatly impeded by the carelessness
and mismanagement of the theatrical authorities,
and when at last all was ready for the first performance, the curtain did not rise till three hours
after the hour announced, and it was two in the
morning before it fell. Nevertheless the audience,
which included the Archduke and his bride, was
enthusiastic in its appreciation, and the opera had
a successful run of nearly thirty nights.

CHAPTER VIII

THE return of Leopold and his son to Salzburg
was a matter rather of necessity than of choice.
The change from the spacious, care-free life they
had been enjoying in Italy to the routine service
of the Archbishop's court in a small provincial
town was a distasteful experience for which reunion with wife and daughter did not adequately
compensate. But the Italian tour had been by no
means a gold-mine, and the precarious state of
the family finances forbade any further absence
from home duties.

The Mozarts resumed their old work at the
Salzburg court, but under a different master.
There had arisen a new king over Egypt which
knew not Joseph. Archbishop Sigismund had died,
and Hieronymus was reigning in his stead. Sigismund was a pious, kindly man, who had a genuine
love of music so far, at any rate, as it could be
used to adorn the services of the Church, and took
a fatherly interest in the young genius whom he
had appointed Konzertmeister. He conducted the
affairs of his court with rigorous economy, and the
musicians attached to it had perforce to acquiesce
in a meagre remuneration, and in severely restric-

ted opportunities for the practice of their art, for
the sake of the small pension that was secured to
them. The new Archbishop was even more parsi-
monious. He had no taste for serious music, and
was much more interested in horses and field
sports and the society of pretty women. It was long
before he realized that there was anything unusual
about the young Konzertmeister whom his predecessor bequeathed to him, but he soon saw that
the boy had an amazingly ready pen and would
respond at once to any demands made on him. So
he continued to pay him the wretched pittance of
one hundred and fifty gulden a year, while exacting the full tale of masses and motets for the service
of the Church and requiring him to produce suit-
able music for special occasions without any extra
remuneration.

Leopold chafed uneasily at the narrowness and
monotony of Salzburg life after all the excitement
of foreign travel, and his paternal pride revolted
against the servile conditions imposed upon his son.
But for financial reasons he dared not assert independence, or do anything that might endanger his
official position at the Archbishop's court. So he
must needs urge Wolfgang to a scrupulous dis-
charge of all the duties laid upon him, while
secretly cherishing the hope of escaping some day
to a wider sphere where the boy's genius could
develop freely and receive the recognition due to
it. Wolfgang needed no urging; music flowed un-
bidden from his pen; and through three laborious
years at Salzburg he produced an unfailing stream
of compositions of all kinds for his master's church
and concert-room. This work was done under
conditions that would have been fatal to any but
composers of real genius, able to assert their
individuality in spite of all obstacles. The court

5

musicians, bound by a narrow tradition, had to keep within the limits of strictly defined forms, and this, while encouraging technical finish, inevitably resulted in a stiff, conventional style of writing. Moreover, the court orchestras, owing to the Archbishop's ill-judged parsimony, were seldom kept up to full strength, and music often had to be produced at short notice for performance by a haphazard combination of instruments from which important elements were missing. This necessity acted only as a spur to Wolfgang's invention. If there was no one to play the viola in the mass which had to be ready for a church festival, he would show how well the music could sound with the part omitted; and he experimented with tireless ingenuity in writing divertimentos and serenades for every conceivable set of instruments, according to the material available at the moment. By this exercise he was doubtless able to strengthen his innate aptitude for handling the different instruments so that each should produce the fullest and most characteristic effect of which it was capable.

As time went on the Mozarts found the atmosphere of Salzburg more and more unsympathetic. Their fellow musicians at the court resented what they regarded as a priggish claim to superior cultivation, and were jealous of Wolfgang's shining talents and of the successes he had won in the outside world. The Archbishop, while always exacting full measure from his Konzertmeister, was ruthless in his criticism of the work so faithfully prepared for him. "You know nothing of your art," he told Wolfgang one day, "and you ought to go to a conservatoire in Italy to learn how to compose." It was the last and crudest of a long series of gibes and insults, and it stung

Leopold to action. He applied to the Archbishop
for an increase of salary for himself and his son
and at the same time for leave to go off on another
foreign tour. The double request was hardly
judicious, and not unnaturally it was roundly
refused; the Archbishop of Salzburg would not
have his subjects "going on begging expeditions."
So an alternative method of escape was devised.
Wolfgang was to resign his situation at the court
and go abroad with his mother in quest of a
more lucrative appointment in the service of
another master. This, if it could be obtained,
would, it was hoped, enable the father and
daughter finally to break loose from Salzburg and
to reunite the family under freer and happier
conditions elsewhere. The Archbishop accepted
his Konzertmeister's resignation with an ill grace,
and, towards the end of September 1777, mother
and son set forth on their travels. Leopold felt
the separation keenly. He could not bring himself to be present at the farewell scene, and in his
distress he even forgot to give the travellers a
parting benediction. When at last he realized
that they were gone, he rushed to the window to
send his blessing after them. But they had passed
through the city gate and were already out of
sight.

It was a discouraging start to a young musician's
journey in quest of fame and fortune. The
undelivered message of paternal affection took a
more prosaic form in the letter that awaited the
travellers on arriving at Munich, their first place
of call. "Money-making," wrote Leopold,
"must engross all your attention, and economy
must be all your care, otherwise a journey is of
no profit; on the contrary, it brings a man into
debt." He was clearly more concerned with the

financial prospects of the tour than with any influence it might have on the development of Wolfgang's musical powers. It was his proud boast that, though poor, he had always a little more than was absolutely necessary—a position that would have satisfied Mr. Micawber—and now his son must learn this great secret of human happiness. Certainly Wolfgang worked with unflagging spirit to achieve what his father insisted was the chief purpose of his expedition. Wherever he went he left no stone unturned to commend himself to the notice of those in authority. At Munich the Elector was kindly and sympathetic; but there was no post he could offer him at present; everything was held by Italian musicians; perhaps if Herr Mozart would travel to Italy and make a name for himself, something might be found for him. Wolfgang modestly pointed out that he had already spent sixteen months in Italy and written three operas there, and he produced his diploma from the Bolognese Academy and a testimonial from Padre Martini; but it was all of no avail. Leopold, when he heard the story, replied with a hint that there were secret enemies at work in Munich and a suggestion that a move should be made to other towns where the mania for Italian musicians did not prevail.

So, after a short stay at Augsburg—Leopold's native town—mother and son proceeded to Mannheim, the seat of the Elector Palatine, whose orchestra, the finest in all Germany, was maintained at so lavish an expense that there was little to spare for the material needs of his unfortunate subjects. Wolfgang was received at Court with every mark of princely favour, and was soon in great request for musical entertainments of all kinds. The Elector listened with growing admiration to his playing, consulted him about the musical training of his children, and persuaded him to give them some lessons on the clavier. But, as usual, these services were rewarded rather by trinkets and caresses than in hard cash. During his stay at Mannheim, Wolfgang was given as many as five watches by his admirers, but the assurance of a settled income was as far off as ever. His brilliant performances gained for him enemies as well as friends, and an indiscreet outburst of sarcastic criticism on the compositions of the Abbé Vogler, the Elector's Kapellmeister, set a powerful influence to work to undermine his position at the Court. In the end the Elector's fair promises and kindly words, which had buoyed him up through months of waiting, gave place to a blunt intimation that he had nothing to offer him at Mannheim.

Leopold, on hearing the news, decided at once that nothing was to be gained by further lingering at Mannheim, and wrote to his son urging an immediate move to Paris. "From Paris," he said, "the name and fame of a man of great talent resounds through all the world. There the nobility treat men of genius with the greatest condescension, esteem, and courtesy; there you may see a manner of life which contrasts most astonishingly with the coarseness of our German cavaliers and their ladies, and there you may perfect yourself in the French tongue." There, the letter continued, he would find many influential friends, notably Baron von Grimm, who would welcome him and do their utmost to promote his interests; Paris was full of keen musical amateurs who would pay him handsomely for lessons on the harpsichord or violin; and what

time was left free from teaching he could devote
to supplying the Parisian market with compositions of every kind—quartet, symphony, song,
opera. But before writing anything for the
French he must study the national taste and
adapt his style to it. For this wordly-wise
counsel Leopold quoted an illustrious precedent.
"Voltaire," he said, "reads his poems to his
friends, listens to their verdict, and alters accord-
ingly. So must Mozart do if he is to make money."

Wolfgang viewed with some misgiving the
prospect of life in Paris on the lines laid down by
his father, and he particularly disliked the idea
of having to bury his creative powers under the
mechanical drudgery of teaching, however well
paid. He found, moreover, the social atmosphere
of the city a good deal less congenial than his
father had led him to expect. It was a very
different Paris from that of his boyish memory
fourteen years before. "The French," he wrote,
"have no longer the *politesse* which formerly distinguished them; their manners now approach
very near to rudeness, and their arrogance is
abominable." He was annoyed, too, at being still
treated rather as an infant prodigy than as a
serious artist. "The people merely pay me compliments and then it is all over; they invite me to
their houses, listen to my playing, and say 'O
c'est un prodige, c'est inconcevable, c'est étonnant';
and then 'adieu.'" The society of his old friend
Grimm was a welcome relief from these humiliat-
ing experiences. From him he could be sure of
receiving sage counsel, a sympathetic hearing to his
contemptuous judgments on French musical taste,
generous hospitality, and a passport to acquaintance with many persons of influence in the artistic
world of Paris. Among the latter was the Duchesse

de Bourbon, who invited Wolfgang to her house and asked him to entertain her guests with some piano-playing. It was a depressing specimen of a Parisian *salon*. The room was vast and unheated, with doors and windows open; at one end of it a miserable rattletrap of a piano, and in the middle a handful of people, with their hostess, sitting round a table and entirely absorbed in drawing. Wolfgang, feeling frozen alike in body and in spirit, played with numb fingers to an audience, as he described it to Grimm, not of men and women, but of walls, chairs, and tables, and now and then the company looked up from their drawing and gave him some languid applause.

Another noble house to which Grimm obtained introduction was that of the Duc de Guines, an enthusiastic musical amateur, who engaged Wolfgang to give lessons in composition to his daughter. It was uphill work, for the girl was lazy and unresponsive, and all that her teacher could get her to do, after long, laborious hours, was to tack on some obvious endings to pieces which he had written out for her. This and a few other teaching engagements secured for him a modest subsistence during his stay in Paris, but his letters to his father are full of complaints at being compelled to spend on his pupils the time and energy that he needed for his own creative work. That work, indeed, could never be set aside. His brain, now as always, was teeming with musical ideas, and whenever he could free himself from his teaching fetters he was writing at his desk. Compositions of all kinds—Church music, concerto, symphony, ballet music, opera—flowed from his pen in quick succession; but to get any of these performed was a much more difficult matter than to write them. Here, as elsewhere, there were hostile influences at work to

thwart the recognition of a rising genius. Wolfgang's chief aim was to get his music performed at
the Concert Spirituel, with whose director, Le
Gros, he was on very friendly terms, but it was only
after months of delay that the new symphony,
which was the most important fruit of his Paris
visit, was put into rehearsal by that famous
orchestra. He sent his father a curious account of
the performance of this work. He told how at a
particular passage in the first movement there was
an outburst of applause; he knew when he wrote
it that it would produce a sensation, so he brought
it in again at the end : the finale he began with an
unexpected *pianissimo,* whereat there was a loud
" Sh ! " from the audience; then a *forte,* which
was greeted with hand-clapping. " After the
symphony," he ended his letter, " I went to the
Palais Royal, ate an ice, said the rosary I had
vowed, and went home." No doubt he did himself an injustice in suggesting that he introduced
deliberate *ad captandum* effects into a serious work.
It was his way of expressing the contempt he felt
for the lowness of French musical taste. He told
his father that as far as music was concerned he
was living among mere brute beasts, and he would
thank Almighty God if he escaped from Paris with
his healthy natural taste unvitiated. " I pray God
daily," he wrote with pious resignation, " to give
me grace to endure here steadfastly, to do honour
to the whole German nation, putting His glory
first, and to grant me to gain fame and money so
that I may be able to help you out of your present
embarrassed circumstances and effect our speedy
reunion, when we may all live together in joy and
prosperity."

But before the happy reunion could come about
there was a gap in the little family circle. In the

early days of July 1778, Frau Anna Mozart died in her son's arms. The blow called forth all that was best and tenderest in Wolfgang's character. His first thought was to spare his father and sister the shock of a sudden announcement. So he sent the news to an old family friend at Salzburg, the Abbé Bullinger, with a request to prepare his father by gentle degrees for the sad tidings. Then he wrote to his father saying that his mother was seriously ill and exhorting him to resign himself calmly to the will of God, whatever the issue might be; he even tried to divert his mind to other things by a lively description of the muddle and incompetence of the rehearsals given to the Paris symphony at the Concert Spirituel. The pathetic little ruse was of no avail—Leopold read only too clearly between the lines, and before Wolfgang's second letter, telling the real news, arrived he had become convinced that the worst had happened.

At the thought of his son motherless and alone in a great unfriendly city, Leopold was filled with anxious foreboding. The streets of Paris after all were not paved with gold, and his hopes of seeing Wolfgang succeed to a post of honour and affluence in a foreign capital were fast fading away. He longed to have him at home again. In one of his letters he had said that it was a kind of martyrdom to him to be told of all the music that his dear son was writing in Paris and to know that he could hear nothing of that which once was his chiefest delight. Life at Salzburg might be cramped and unenterprising, but there at any rate Wolfgang would be among his own people, and safe, under the watchful guidance of his father, from the seductive wiles of flatterers and charlatans. Moreover, the Archbishop was beginning to realize how much he had lost in parting with his Konzertmeister, and

was even making tentative efforts to recapture him
for his service. A timely vacancy had occurred in
the establishment of the court, and Leopold used
all his diplomatic skill to secure his son's reappoint-
ment to fill it. In the end, satisfactory terms were
arranged; Wolfgang was to be paid a salary of five
hundred florins in his new post, and whenever he
wished to write an opera he might have leave to go
abroad. So at the end of September 1778 he left
Paris and once more turned his steps homeward.

The tour from the point of view of material
profit had been disappointingly unfruitful, but
during its course three things happened to Mozart
which had an important influence on his future
career.

First, at Augsburg he made the acquaintance of
Andreas Stein, famous maker of organs and harpsi-
chords, who was now applying his inventive skill
to the mechanism of the new instrument that was
just coming into vogue. Three of these " pianofortes," as they were called, stood in Stein's ware-
house, and Mozart spent long hours playing upon
them and probing the secrets of their workmanship.
A world of new possibilities seemed to be opening
out for him. Even his mother noticed a remarkable change. " He plays quite differently," she
reported to her husband, " from what he does at
Salzburg, for there are pianofortes here and you
never heard anything like the way he manages
them; everyone that hears him declares that his
equal is not to be found." Henceforth it was as a
pianist that he was to be chiefly known to the
world; he never played the violin in public again,
while with the pianoforte he went from strength to
strength; on it he raised extemporization to the
level of a fine art that stirred and enchanted all

who heard it, and the piano concerto became the
vehicle for some of his finest and most characteristic musical utterances.

The second and still more important event of
the tour was Mozart's introduction, at Mannheim,
to the finest body of orchestral players in Europe.
The Elector Palatine may have had obvious short-
comings as a ruler, but at least he had a claim to
grateful recognition for the part he played in
creating and maintaining the Mannheim orchestra.
Burney had heard this famous band some years
before and admired the delicacy of their playing,
with its subtle gradations of light and shade : it
was here, as he put it, that *crescendo* and *diminu-
endo* had birth. Since then the orchestra had come
under the inspiration of a conductor of genius,
Cannabich, and had been wrought into a combination of rare excellence. It was a revelation to
Mozart. He said Cannabich was the best musical
director he had ever seen, and marvelled at the
perfect discipline he had achieved by the exercise
of an unquestioned personal authority—a contrast
indeed to the slovenly performances of the Salzburg musicians. At Mannheim, too, there were
clarinets to be heard that added fascinating new
colours to the body of orchestral tone. Mozart at
once took this instrument to his heart, and his
writing for it—culminating in the exquisite quintet
for clarinet and strings eleven years later—was
always marked by a peculiar mastery.

But at Mannheim there was a more potent
attraction than Cannabich and his band, and here
occurred the third of the important events—
Mozart fell in love with Aloysia Weber. He had
already had some gentle flutters of the heart. Six
years before, when he was fifteen, he had confessed
to his sister that he was passionately attached to a

young Salzburg lady, " a nameless beauty, of un-
speakable emotions." Later, on a visit to Augsburg, he carried on a flirtation with his cousin
Marianne. " We two," he told his father, " suit
each other exactly, for she is just a little wicked,"
and he amused himself by writing her ardent love-
letters with a plentiful seasoning of coarse jokes
and rhymes. But the affair with Aloysia was much
more serious. She was the second of four daughters
of Fridolin Weber, a needy musician employed as
prompter at the Mannheim theatre, and already,
at the age of sixteen, the possessor of a voice of rare
beauty and freshness, that was destined in after
years to raise her to the highest rank of operatic
singers. Mozart yielded readily to the enchant-
ment. Splendid visions floated before him. He
would write grand operas, with the principal parts
specially designed for Aloysia and with elaborate
arias and scenas to display the glories of her voice;
armed with these, he would go with the Weber
family on a triumphal progress through Italy, and
together Wolfgang and Aloysia would conquer the
world. He announced the daring project to his
father in a letter which discreetly laid stress on the
domestic virtues of the Weber household and the
" inexpressible pleasure he derived from having
made the acquaintance of true-hearted Catholic
and Christian people." But Leopold was not to be
won over by soft words. He could hardly bring
himself to write what he thought of such an insane
proposal. The idea of his son gallivanting about
Italy with a penniless musician and his daughters
when there was serious work to be done, and fame
and fortune awaiting him in Paris, filled him with
speechless horror; to allow it would expose him to
the derision of his master, the Archbishop, and all
Salzburg. Mozart bowed his head to the storm

with childlike submission; "God first and then papa" was still his rule of life. There was a tearful leave-taking from Aloysia and her family, and Leopold was able to thank God from his heart that his son had escaped a great danger.

A few months later Mozart broke his homeward journey from Paris to visit the Webers at Munich, where they, with the rest of the Mannheim musicians, were now settled. He had asked his Augsburg cousin to meet him there, hinting that she might have an important part to play. The girl came, but the part she had to play was to console a broken heart. Aloysia met her lover with cold indifference; she hardly seemed to recognize him. He saw at once that his happy dream was over; he sat down at the piano and burst out into a bitter little song: "Ich lass das Mädel gern, das mich nicht will."

Aloysia had rejected Mozart, but she never forgot his music. The fine arias that he wrote for her, in which he put on her lips the expression of his own tender feelings, were treasures that she never tired of displaying to the world, and as a mature artist she was destined to win the most signal triumphs of her career in *Die Entführung* and *Don Giovanni*.

CHAPTER IX

Idomeneo at Munich—Mozart goes to Vienna in the Archbishop's train—revolts and leaves his service.

THE year 1779 found Mozart established once more in the service of the Archbishop at Salzburg. The experiences through which he had just passed had wrought a significant change in him; the stage of precocious boyhood was left behind, and he stood on the threshold of manhood, conscious of enlarged powers and fired with more daring ambitions. In the hours that could be spared from his routine duties he applied himself with a fresh ardour to the study of dramatic composition, and to the devising of new modes of expression in that branch of the musical art which always stood first in his affections. He was soon to have an opportunity of putting his powers to the test. In the autumn of 1780 he received from the Elector Palatine, now settled with his Mannheim orchestra at Munich, a commission to compose a grand opera for the ensuing carnival on the subject of *Idomeneo,* a counterpart from Greek mythology of the biblical story of Jephtha's vow. The agreed conditions of his service at the Salzburg court left him free for an enterprise of this kind, and he set out for Munich with all speed. There the prospects were not altogether favourable. Among the singers cast for the principal parts of the opera were Del Prato, a broken-down male soprano, who had

never before appeared on the stage, and Anton
Raaff, the once famous tenor, but now nearly
seventy years old, with an attenuated voice incapable of sustaining notes of any length. On the
other hand, there was the great Cannabich and an
orchestra of the finest quality eager to welcome
the music of a master of genius and to find in it
material worthy of their highest skill. The difficulties no less than the advantages of the situation
stimulated Mozart to a white heat of creative
energy. Raaff had to be provided with lightly
scored airs that would allow him to display the
faded beauty of his voice without making too great
demands on his slender reserves of breath; Del
Prato, who had no more experience of opera than
the boys in the cathedral choir at Salzburg, had
to be drilled laboriously through the simplest
passages; and the motley set of principals could not
be induced to combine with any effect in concerted
numbers. But for these troubles the orchestra was
a rich compensation, and, with such an instrument
ready to his hand, Mozart could give free rein to
his exuberant fancy. He worked at the score with
a peculiar intensity and exhilaration, and in two
months *Idomeneo*—his first dramatic masterpiece
—was completed. On the 29th of January, 1781,
the opera was performed with brilliant success, and
among the enthusiastic audience present was a
little company of Salzburgers who had come to
Munich to witness their fellow-townsman's
triumph.

The happy weeks of liberty at Munich were
over, and it was time for the Archbishop's servant
to put on his chains again. He received a peremp-
tory summons to follow in his master's train to
Vienna, where on the death of Maria Theresa her
son Joseph had recently succeeded to the imperial

throne; and there Hieronymus of Salzburg was in duty bound to pay his respects to the new sovereign. Mozart was glad enough to be in Vienna again; but he soon began to chafe at the menial position in which he found himself in the Archbishop's household and at the petty restrictions on his liberty to which he was subjected. He described to his father the company he kept at the court dinner-table—two valets, the controller, the confectioner, and two cooks; the valets sat at the head, but he had at least the honour of being placed above the cooks. He could hardly move hand or foot without his master's leave. He was not allowed to give public concerts, or to accept the frequent invitations he received from his friends among the Viennese nobility to play at their musical soirées. The Archbishop might want a special piece of work to be done at a moment's notice, and his servant must be always at hand to do his bidding. Mozart particularly resented the loss of opportunity to commend himself to the notice of the Emperor Joseph, a genuine lover of music, as he knew, with a special taste for fugues which it would have been a pleasure for a loyal subject to gratify.

The position was clearly intolerable, and Mozart's resentment soon broke out into open rebellion. The Archbishop was greatly annoyed at not being invited by the Emperor to his summer residence, and in a huff he ordered his household either to return to Salzburg, or to stay on in Vienna at their own charges. This was the breaking-point, and Mozart resolved to strike for freedom. He had never been a respecter of persons; his manners, even in the presence of grandees of the German Courts, were always easy-going and familiar, and quite lacking in the outward marks

of deference accustomed to be paid to them.
Though he lived outside history, and rarely
troubled himself about its making, he was, without
knowing it, a true son of the revolutionary period
in Europe, and now, in his revolt against the pre-
tentious authority of a fossil feudalism, he was a
forerunner of the great movement which took
shape in France a few years later. In a significant
phrase he spoke of the Archbishop acting as a
Lichtschirm to him, a screen that shut out from
the growing plant the sunlight and fresh air that
were necessary to its life. At all costs he must
escape from this imprisonment, even though it
involved the sacrifice of the salary and pension
secured to him as Konzertmeister at Salzburg and
dependence on the uncertain favours of the
Viennese public. In Vienna he would at least be
free to work out his own musical salvation; there
he had many friends and patrons of high rank and
influence, who all encouraged him in his adven-
turous bid for liberty; he would be able to supplement the profits of public performance and
concerts by giving lessons in the houses of the rich,
and thus be assured of earning an adequate livelihood.

The Archbishop accepted his Konzertmeister's
resignation with contemptuous indifference.
Mozart described to his father the unpleasant
interviews that he had with his master on the
subject, how the taunts and insults which " this
wonderful man of God " heaped on him made
him so ill that he was forced to leave the opera-
house in the middle of a performance and reel
home like a drunkard in the street, and how the
final ceremony of leave-taking was speeded up by
a parting kick from Count Arco, the Archbishop's
steward. " If I had to beg my bread," he said,

6

" I would never serve such a lord again. Now fare
you well, and be glad that you have not a coward
for a son." Leopold, however, was less impressed
by the bravery of his son's action than by the
dangerous financial consequences likely to ensue
from it. To exchange an assured, if modest,
salaried position at the Salzburg court for a precarious life of independence in Vienna, seemed to
him the height of improvidence, the first step on
the road to ruin. He even went so far as to demand
that Mozart should recall his resignation. But he
forgot that the boy whose steps he had guided
from the earliest years was now a high-spirited
young man of twenty-five, and for the first time
his fatherly counsel met with rebuff. In the end
he brought himself to a grudging acquiescence to
heap reproaches on his son's head and to distract
him with dismal forebodings of the consequences
of his rash act. The dispute, indeed, left a per-
manent mark of bitterness on the relations between
father and son : it was part—the most painful part
—of the price that Mozart had to pay for his
freedom.

CHAPTER X

Mozart's life in Vienna—his friends—*Die Entführung aus dem Serail—Entführung aus dem Auge Gottes*—Marriage with Constanze Weber—visits Salzburg with his wife—Leopold's return visit to Vienna—his death.

FOR the remaining ten years of Mozart's life Vienna was his home, and here in the joy of his newly gained freedom his artistic powers blossomed forth in their full splendour. The works of his earlier years, astonishing indeed in their profusion, in their technical finish, and in the knowledge they displayed of all that was best in the music of his contemporaries, were yet essentially those of a boy; they were not precocious in the sense that they seemed like the productions of a mature and experienced artist. He was then not old enough to have a story to tell, a nature to reveal. Now, in Vienna, he was a man, whose path lay in shadow as well as sunshine, free to put into his music his full individuality, as it was coloured and moulded by the joys and sorrows of the passing years. So it was that in this period almost everything that he wrote was a masterpiece, marked by that combination of sensitiveness and delicacy of perception with an unerring sense of proportion, the perfect union of form and feeling, in which Mozart is supreme among the world's masters of music.

The shadows were to deepen as time went on, but for the present life was bright and exhilarating.

From the Emperor downwards, all the fashionable world of Vienna gave a warm welcome to the young genius who had come to make his home in their midst. Chief among his friends and admirers was the charming Countess Thun, famous for her musical receptions, which were attended by all the great of the land, and herself an accomplished pianist. Burney spoke highly of her playing, and called her "St. Cecilia of Vienna," though she protested to him that her skill was not what it had been, since each of the six children she had borne had carried away something of her musical power. Other influential friends were Lichnowsky, a son-in-law of Countess Thun, who took lessons from Mozart and later was honoured by some of Beethoven's works being dedicated to him; Baron von Swieten, superintendent of the royal music library, whose devotion to Bach and Handel did much to inspire Mozart to a closer study of their works; Prince Galitzin, the Russian Ambassador, who engaged Mozart to play the clavier at all his concerts, and sent his carriage to take him to and fro; and the gay and brilliant Baroness von Waldstäd-ten, who was the first to take him under her wing and to whom at times of difficulty he would often turn for sympathy and help.

The Emperor Joseph II was a keen musician, with a fine bass voice and some skill as an instrumental performer. He had a decided preference for Italian music, spoke slightingly of Haydn and his "tricks," and at the chamber concerts which took place in his apartments every afternoon the works of native composers were generally excluded. In regard to Mozart's music, he affected an attitude of Olympian impartiality between Italian partisans belittling the rival who they knew would soon beat them out of the field and enlightened friends like Countess Thun, who would fain persuade him that the young man was a heaven-sent genius. An Italian champion in the person of Clementi, the famous virtuoso, had just arrived in Vienna, and the Emperor invited him to a contest of skill with Mozart in clavier playing. Mozart told his father that Clementi was a mere mechanic without a farthing's-worth of taste or feeling, but he paid him the compliment of exercising his fingers vigorously before the encounter. The lists were set; " La Santa Chiesa Cattolica," cried the Emperor as a signal to the Roman Clementi to begin; then, with less formality, " Allons, d'rauf los," to Mozart. It was a comprehensive test—in playing of set pieces, sight-reading, extemporization—but the result was not long in doubt. Joseph had laid a wager on Mozart's success with the Russian Grand Duchess, who was then his guest at the palace, and he won comfortably.

Mrs. Thrale, the friend of Dr. Johnson, said of the Emperor that he was a stranger upon principle to the joys of confidence and friendship, and masked his cold-heartedness and insincerity under a flattering surface. However that may be, his demeanour towards Mozart was cordiality itself, though it was a long time before his benevolence took any material shape. He succeeded at any rate in winning the affectionate loyalty of one who was by no means prone to a deferential respect for those in high places.

Mozart had not been long in Vienna before he was given an opportunity of employing his now fully matured powers on an important dramatic work and at the same time striking an effective blow on behalf of the musical art of his native land. The Emperor Joseph, in spite of his personal preference for Italian music, was anxious on patriotic grounds to establish a German opera-house in his capital. Three years before—in 1778— he had arranged for the Burgtheater to be re-opened and used for this purpose, and on this stage a few specimens of light German opera— *Singspiel,* as this native form was called—had been performed. But these were mostly poor stuff, the work of local mediocrities, and Joseph's laudable enterprise was languishing for want of genius to direct it. Fortunately, a genius had lately come to Vienna, and to Mozart the theatre management turned for help in their time of need. They offered him the libretto of an ordinary *Singspiel*— *Die Entführung aus dem Serail.* He at once saw the possibilities of it, set to work to revise and largely rewrite the text, and from this slender material produced a true German comic opera in which for the first time German sentiment and emotion found dramatic expression at the hands of a great artist. In this and every opera, as he was careful to insist, the music was to be everything and the poetry only its obedient handmaid; he was a long way from the position of Gluck, who said that when he sat down to write an opera he en-deavoured before all things to forget that he was a musician. It was, indeed, Mozart's supreme achievement to combine a delicate sense of dramatic fitness and subtle delineation of character with unswerving loyalty to the paramount claims of pure musical beauty.

Die Entführung was produced in the summer of 1782 amid much demonstration of popular approval, though some grumbles and sneers were still to be heard from supporters of the old Italian tradition. The Emperor himself was puzzled rather than pleased by the unfamiliar richness of Mozart's score; " too fine for our ears, my dear Mozart, and an immense number of notes," was his summary criticism. " Just as many notes, your majesty, as are necessary," was the composer's terse reply.

Meantime his thoughts had been turning towards the prospect of another *Entführung—Aus dem Auge Gottes,* the name of the house where the Weber family were settled in Vienna. Aloysia, his first love, was now married to the actor Lange, and her place in Mozart's affections was taken by her sister Constanze. He was careful, however, in writing to his father, to insist that the marriage he contemplated with her would be based on prudence rather than on passion. " Aloysia," he said, " is a false, unprincipled woman, and a coquette. My dear good Constanze is the martyr of the family, and on that very account, perhaps, the best-natured, the cleverest—in a word, the best of them all. She is not beautiful—far from it—*but she understands housekeeping.*" The news was a heavy blow to Leopold. Years before, when his son was going to visit Paris, he had warned him to beware of the wiles of the female sex, and had told him that it depended on his own sense whether he was to end his days in squalor and poverty, herded together with his wife in a room full of squalling brats on a sack of straw, or spend a Christian life, full of honour, pleasure and profit, and die respected by all the world, leaving his family well provided for. Now, when Mozart announced his betrothal to the daughter of a poor musician, his father was haunted again by his vision of the squalling brats and the sack of straw; marriage, he protested, without an assured income meant ruin and misery, and he was convinced that his son had been entangled by a designing mother and daughter in an alliance that held out no

promise of happiness or comfort. Wolfgang's airy
speculations on the possibilities of a brighter
financial future left his father quite unconvinced,
and his urgent entreaties for consent to his marriage met for some time with a stubborn refusal.
There was trouble, too, with Frau Weber, an ill-
tempered woman who drank more than was good
for her and whose scoldings of her daughters for
their refusal to touch wine caused domestic scenes
that were an unpleasant feature in Mozart's visits
to his lady at *Das Auge Gottes*. She objected
strongly on moral grounds to Constanze's associa-
tion with Baroness von Waldstädten, who had
warmly espoused the lovers' cause and had allowed
them to meet at her house when they liked, and
even threatened to send the police to fetch the girl
home. Mozart at last took the law into his own
hands. With the help of the friendly Baroness, the
Entführung was accomplished, and on the 4th of
August, 1782, Wolfgang and Constanze became
man and wife. Leopold in the end gave a grudging
consent, but the letter conveying the paternal blessing actually did not arrive till the day after the
wedding ceremony, and it contained, besides the
blessing, a warning that Wolfgang, having brought
himself into a position when he could no longer
help to restore the family fortunes, must neither
now nor at any future time reckon upon his father
for support, and a request that this state of things
might be made clear to his bride.

The marriage was an assertion of independence
which sorely puzzled and wounded Leopold. He
was never really reconciled to it, and Mozart's
efforts to establish friendly relations between his
wife and his father met with little success. Corres-
pondence between the two continued, but the
letters became less frequent, and there is a subtle

but unmistakable change in their tone. Henceforth
Leopold must resign the charge of his son into
God's hands. " I have done my duty as a father,"
he wrote to a friend, " and now there is no resource
to me but to leave him (as he has so willed it) to
himself, and to pray the Almighty to bestow my
paternal blessing on him and not to withdraw His
Divine mercy."

Mozart felt deeply the estrangement from his
father which his marriage had brought about, and
he was anxious as soon as possible to heal the
breach by taking his wife to visit his old home at
Salzburg. But money difficulties, that were to cast
an ever-deepening shadow over his life, were even
now showing themselves, and some troublesome
claims had to be satisfied before the journey could
be undertaken. Salzburg itself was not drawing
him; nothing that he ever said or wrote suggests
that he felt any affection or admiration for the
delightful town where he was born and brought
up. He cared for no art but his own, he was not
very sensitive to the beauties of natural scenery,
and the charms of Salzburg were obliterated in
his mind by memories of the galling servitude that
he had suffered there.

Mozart and his wife arrived in Salzburg in July
1783, and stayed there with Leopold for three
months. His first care was to complete the mass
which he had begun earlier in the year as a thank-
offering for his marriage. This work was the finest
of its kind that he ever wrote, and in its breadth
of style and solemnity of feeling was on an altogether different level from the perfunctory specimens
of Church music that he turned out in earlier years
at the bidding of the Archbishop. The mass was
duly performed in St. Peter's Church, and Frau
Constanze, whose voice was a pale reflection of

her famous sister's, sang the soprano solos—her only recorded appearance as a public performer. Other fruits of Mozart's Salzburg holiday were two Italian operas, left incomplete, in which, with an eye on the prevailing Viennese taste, he thought out afresh the problems of dramatic composition and practised the hand that was soon to produce *Figaro* and *Don Giovanni*. He found time, too, for a characteristic act of kindness to an old friend. Michael Haydn, Kapellmeister at Salzburg, and still condemned to waste his talents in the cramping service of the Archbishop, was just now seriously ill and quite unfit for work. An order came to him from his master to produce a set of duets for violin and viola by a certain day, with the threatened loss of salary in case of failure. Mozart at once came to his rescue. He set to work himself on the duets with all speed, handed them to his friend, and told him he might use them as his own handiwork for any purpose he required.

As a means of establishing friendly relations between his father and his wife, Mozart's visit to his old home was less successful. His letter to Leopold after returning to Vienna was not very cordial; like many a " Collins " of modern times, it was a good deal taken up with a detailed description of the journey, and it ended rather stiffly by thanking his father for the favours he and his wife had received and asking that the length of their stay might be forgiven.

Some months later, in the spring of 1785, Leopold paid a return visit to his son and daughter-in-law in Vienna, and here, though he was now failing in health and much troubled with attacks of gout, he spent a happy six weeks. Now he saw with delight and pride how the boy whose early steps he had guided had grown to the full stature of genius. He went regularly to the subscription concerts that Mozart was giving at this time, listened with tears in his eyes to the new beauties of the piano concertos that had been written for the occasion, heard the audience's tumult of applause and the Emperor's cry of "Bravo, Mozart" as the composer left the platform. Characteristically, he was concerned as much with his son's economic position as with his musical fame. He cast a critical eye over the young couple's housekeeping arrangements and found, so far as eating and drinking were concerned, no sign of extravagance; he concluded, indeed, that if they exercised due care, and if there were no debts to pay, they could now put aside a substantial amount of savings against a rainy day. Mozart, however, was incurably unbusinesslike, and his father was constantly reproaching him for the carelessness with which he would let his best written compositions slip out of his hands and allow others to reap the profits that should have accrued to himself. Perhaps he was beginning to realize that for all the anxious care that he had devoted to his son's training he had never succeeded in teaching him habits of ordinary prudence in the affairs of everyday life. At any rate, he saw that he could not now hope to resume the old intimate relations, and he dismissed as impracticable the proposal that he should spend the remainder of his days with his son in Vienna. Towards the end of March 1785 he went back to Salzburg, and father and son never met again. Two years later news of Leopold's serious illness drew from Mozart an affectionate letter of tender solicitude in which he told his father of the consolation he had derived from the Masonic teaching about death as the true friend of mankind, the fulfilment of the real purpose of

human life. In May 1787 Leopold died, a lonely,
saddened old man. He had lived long enough to
know that his son was secure of a place among the
great figures of musical history, and he was merci-
fully spared from witnessing the final catastrophe—
which his own strict guardianship in earlier years
had unwittingly helped to bring about—when the
man whom he had hoped to see prosperous and
independent, " at the head of a comfortable
Christian household," was entangled in the toils of
moneylenders and swindlers, and barely earning
enough, by constant overwork, to keep body and
soul together.

CHAPTER XI

The last ten years—Mozart's creative activity—his method
of composition—friendship with Haydn.

In the free and stimulating atmosphere of Vienna,
Mozart led a life of astonishing activity. With a
wife and, soon, a growing family dependent on
him for support, and with no assured income from
an official appointment, he could not afford to miss
any opportunity that promised even the smallest
financial return. The whole morning of every day
till two o'clock, he tells us, was taken up with
lesson-giving; it was only in the evening that he
could write anything, and even that time was fre-
quently interrupted by invitations to play at
concerts and musical parties. On Sundays he
generally gave performances in his own house, or
he would go round to Baron von Swieten's, where
nothing was played but Handel and Bach, and he
first began to know and to love the Forty-Eight
preludes and fugues. Nor was he a stranger to the
lighter side of Viennese life. Michael Kelly, the
Irish singer, who came to fulfil an engagement at
the Imperial opera-house in 1784, and made great
friends with Mozart, says that at that time the
whole of Vienna was dancing mad; he describes
how he met Mozart at a party, and listened to his
wonderful piano playing; how, after supper, there
was dancing, in which he joined with the utmost
zest and gaiety, and declared that his real taste lay
in that art rather than in music. Another source

of recreation was in the festivities and friendly gatherings of the Masonic Lodge of which Mozart was enrolled a brother soon after his arrival in Vienna. Freemasonry with its ideals of brotherhood, kindliness to the sad and suffering, and independence of priestly domination, made an especial appeal to him; he remained throughout faithful to the Order, despite the neglect and persecution which it suffered in later years, and its essential spirit was enshrined in the last and greatest of his operas.

Yet, amid all these manifold distractions of work and amusement, Mozart found time in ten crowded years to produce a long series of works which are among the richest treasures of the world's musical inheritance. The list includes, besides the four great operas, all the finest of his compositions for various combinations of instruments—the ten best string quartets, the two piano quartets, the piano quintet, the seven last, and finest, of his symphonies, the last seventeen piano concertos, the string quintets, the clarinet quintet, and the clarinet concerto. Add to these a large number of pieces of smaller scale or of less serious significance and the full tale of his separate compositions in these years comes to more than two hundred. It is not surprising that such immense creative activity, combined with all the work that he was driven to do to earn a livelihood, should have overtaxed his strength and brought him to collapse and an early death. He said himself that he often worked so hard that he did not know whether his head was on or off. It is astonishing that compositions produced under such pressure should show so few signs of haste or carelessness. No doubt there is, to some extent, even in Mozart's mature work, an acceptance of current musical conventions both of form and idea, and a tendency to repeat well-worn phrases and cadences. But in the whole range it would be difficult to point to a single movement where there is any looseness of structure, any uncertainty in thematic treatment, any imperfect balance of instrumental tone. Nor was he content merely to produce faultless specimens in the established forms that lay ready to his hand. He contributed notably to the formal development of the classical concerto, and handled this kind of composition with the utmost freedom and richness of invention. So also with the string quartet and the string quintet; he enlarged and deepened their range of expression, and in the set dedicated to Haydn, and still more strikingly in the G minor quintet—perhaps his greatest achievement in chamber music—there is a note of intimate personal feeling unheard before. In the fifth of these quartets there is an air with variations in which for the first time the variations are reflexions or meditations on the theme instead of mere formal embellishments of it: and the last of them begins with a harmonic progression of such daring originality that it sounds startling even to our modern ears. A contemporary critic spoke of this passage as "the delightful expression of the doctrine of necessary evil, founded on the insufficiency of all finite things"; Sarti, the operatic composer, in a venomous pamphlet, described it as barbarous; and when Count Grassalcovich, a prominent musical connoisseur in Vienna, was having the six quartets performed at his house, he was so convinced that many wrong notes were played that when the parts were handed to him showing that no mistake had been made he tore them up on the spot. The truth is that the spirit of independence which had driven Mozart to break loose from the

restrictions of the Salzburg court was now showing
itself in his music; he was beginning to speak in a
new language which sounded strange to his contemporaries, and he experienced the usual fate of
the artistic pioneer—misunderstanding, neglect,
and a pitifully small measure of material reward.
When, in 1784, in fulfilment of a commission from
Hoffmeister, the Leipzig publisher, he produced
the G minor piano quartet as the first of a series,
he was greeted with a petulant outburst—" Write
more popularly," said Hoffmeister, " or I can
neither print nor pay for anything more of yours."
" Then may the devil take me," replied the composer, " but I will write nothing more and go
hungry," and the commission was summarily
broken off. Mozart was not to be turned by
ignorant criticism or clamour from pursuit of the
ideal that he had set before himself. He had all
the self-confidence of genius; he knew that in the
work he was doing in these years in Vienna he was
reaching up to greater heights than he had known
before. He told his father that the quintet for
piano and wind—one of the earliest of his mature
masterpieces—was the best thing he had ever
composed. The date of this was 1784, and in
that year he began to keep a list of his works, with
the initial themes and date of completion in each
case. This he continued regularly until his last illness—a sure proof on the part of one naturally so
careless and unmethodical that he knew he was
making music destined to endure.

Mozart's ability to produce an immense number
of highly finished works of art under conditions
which to the ordinary mortal would have been
intolerably distracting was probably due in great
measure to his singular method of composition, if
indeed one mystery can be said to explain another.

His musical ideas seem to have matured and taken their final shape within his mind, so that when he came to the act of writing he was not so much composing as remembering what was already composed. Hence the appearance of his manuscripts, with no emendations or alterations, no sign of a first rough draft, as in the case of Beethoven, passing by laborious correction into the form finally approved. He could survey a finished work of his imagination as one can look at a picture—not as a succession of parts or phrases, but as a unified whole. So we may think of him going about his business, with his mind, as he once described it to his father, steeped in music the whole day long, while things of beauty were being conceived and fashioned within him; and then, in the evening, putting these creatures of his fancy into written shape. The act of writing was rapid and unfaltering, and was often carried on in the intervals of other activities, or while people were talking or making music round him. Such distractions, indeed, were a stimulus rather than an impediment to the creative process. When he was composing he liked his wife to sit by him and tell him funny stories : he wrote *Don Giovanni* in a friend's garden, to the accompaniment of lively conversation and quoit-playing, jumping up from the desk when the turn came for his throw; and one of the loveliest numbers in *Die Zauberflöte* was jotted down between the strokes of a game of billiards. Strangest of all he could write out one piece while another was taking shape in his brain : there is a letter to his sister, enclosing a manuscript of a prelude and fugue for her edification with the two sections in reverse order; this he explained by saying that he had thought out the prelude while writing down the fugue which he had already composed.

7

There was indeed an element of the miraculous in Mozart's story. In his early days he had been exploited as the infant prodigy, and to the very end of his life there clung to his name a contemptuous suspicion, a recollection of the useless display of mere precocious childish talent, which often obscured the shining achievements of his mature genius.

Through these years in Vienna, there was one friend, at any rate, to whom Mozart could always look for sympathy and encouragement. He had become acquainted with Joseph Haydn's work several years before, during a visit to Vienna in 1773, and had then written some string quartets in which the old master's influence can clearly be traced. Now, in the winter of 1781–2, the two men came into personal contact, and were soon bound together by a strong tie of mutual admiration. In age they were twenty-four years apart, and were widely different in state and fortune: Haydn, under the wise protection of his patron, Prince Esterhazy, pursuing his art in leisure and tranquillity at Eisenstadt; Mozart, recently set free from the galling restraints of his service at Salzburg, and now in a position of precarious independence, impelled to do his creative work in the intervals of wearisome lesson-giving and incessant public performance. But in both alike there glowed the divine fire, and both were unswervingly faithful to the highest ideals that they knew. The security of Haydn's position never relaxed his artistic fibre or impaired his industry: Mozart, with uncertain prospects and the constant menace of poverty, never lowered his standard or sought for profit by any unworthy concession to the popular taste. It was a pure and happy friendship, unsullied by any taint of jealous rivalry. Mozart acknowledged that Haydn had taught him how to write quartets, and the pupil paid the master an immortal tribute by dedicating to him the six masterpieces that he wrote in this form. These he said were the fruits of long and painful study, and he entrusted them to one whose example had inspired them, and upon whose protection and indulgence towards them he could confidently rely. Haydn, for his part, repaid his devotion with unstinted generosity. The master, indeed, did not disdain to sit at the pupil's feet, and in his later string quartets, and especially in the noble set of symphonies that he wrote for Salomon in London after he had bidden farewell to his friend for the last time, there is a new richness of texture, a greater rhythmic freedom, and a wider range of emotional expression, which were undoubtedly the fruits of his study of Mozart's music. He was a frequent guest at the musical parties in Mozart's lodgings, where new compositions were tried over and submitted to the master's kindly criticism. Here he would listen with unfeigned delight to his young friend's piano-playing, the beauty of which, as he said in after years, he could never forget. Here, when Leopold Mozart was in Vienna on a visit to his son in the early spring of 1785, Haydn was invited to meet him, and was entertained with a performance of the three latest of the quartets which had just been dedicated to him. The noble music moved him profoundly, and turning to Leopold he said, " I declare before God, as a man of honour, that your son is the greatest composer of whom I have ever heard."

CHAPTER XII

Italian opera—Mozart and Da Ponte—*Figaro*—*Don Giovanni*—*Così fan tutte*.

THE Emperor's scheme of establishing German opera in Vienna had been powerfully aided, as we have seen, by the popular triumph of *Die Entführung*. But it was a flash in the pan. The theatre managers quarrelled with Mozart because he refused to set a wretched libretto that they offered him, and they resolved thenceforward to carry on their business without the co-operation of the one man who could have secured its success. It was a hopeless task. With nothing but inferior musical material to draw upon, the German theatre soon languished and died; the Italian party resumed its former ascendancy, while its leader, Salieri, the pupil of Gluck, enjoyed a petty triumph in the momentary discomfiture of the rival who threatened to dethrone him. Mozart, for his part, accepted the situation philosophically, and he permitted himself so far to concede to the popular fashion by choosing Italian libretti for the three operas which mark the summit of his achievement in this art. In *Figaro, Don Giovanni,* and *Così fan tutte* there is indeed nothing distinctively Italian but the language; there is no sign of their author's yielding to the claims of an outworn convention or faltering in the pursuit of the ideals of dramatic composition which he had set before himself. Through them all the master's individual touch is sure and unerring—in the vivid depicting of each dramatic situation as it occurs by every appropriate device of rhythm and orchestral colour; in the delicate discrimination of the characters as they move across the scene; above all in the gems of lovely melody that sparkle on every page of the score.

Among the notable men who were living in Vienna at this time was the strange figure of Lorenzo da Ponte. By birth a Venetian Jew, he had received Christian baptism at an early age, and after some years of training at a religious seminary, which were spent for the most part in acquiring a proficiency in Latin and Italian verse-making, he had been admitted to priest's orders. He had adopted the habit without the moral standards of his new religion : in Venice and elsewhere he made himself notorious by many amorous escapades, and by publishing libellous satires on persons in authority; and after many adventures he had at last found refuge in Vienna, and there obtained the post of poet to the Imperial theatre. It was a chance meeting with Mozart, so he tells us in his memoirs, that enabled him to bring into the light a priceless jewel that lay buried in the bowels of the earth. " I can never remember without exultation," he wrote, " that it was to my per-severance and firmness alone that Europe and the world in great part owe the exquisite vocal compositions of that admirable genius." This was certainly putting it rather high, but it is undeniable that Da Ponte did a great service to the cause of art by providing Mozart with three specimens of that rare article—a really effective and well-written opera libretto. The book for the first of the three operas originated in the composer's own suggestion. He had heard the story of Beaumarchais' comedy, *Le*

Mariage de Figaro, how its revolutionary tone and
daring freedom of speech had so horrified Louis
XVI that for a long time he vetoed its performance,
how the King in the end yielded to the combined
force of public opinion and the entreaties of Marie
Antoinette and the piece was performed amid a
riot of popular enthusiasm. It occurred to him
that the adaptation of a play with such a stormy
and exciting career, which Napoleon had described
as "the Revolution already in action," would
make an effective opera libretto, and he pressed
the idea on Da Ponte. There was a difficulty, however, in that the Emperor Joseph had, like Louis,
forbidden the performance of Beaumarchais' work
at the German theatre. Da Ponte decided to take
the risk : he set himself to the task, and as fast as
he wrote the words, Mozart set them to music. In
six weeks the whole was completed. Da Ponte
went himself to present it to the Emperor; he
assured him that all politics had been excluded
from the opera, and everything that might offend
good taste or public decency; as for the music it
seemed to him "marvellously beautiful." Joseph's
apprehensions were allayed; he graciously said that
he would rely on the poet's taste for the music and
on his wisdom for the morality, and gave orders
that *Le Nozze di Figaro* should be put into
rehearsal forthwith. A strong company of singers
was engaged, all Italian save Michael Kelly, the
Irish tenor, and Nancy Storace, the English
soprano; and Kelly tells how he and each of them
had the inspiring experience of being instructed in
every detail of their parts by the composer himself.
The first performance of *Figaro* took place on the
1st of May, 1786, and we have Kelly's pretty
picture of Mozart as he saw him on that memorable evening, in his crimson pelisse and gold-laced

cocked hat, "his little animated countenance
lighted up with the glowing rays of genius, as
impossible to describe as it would be to paint sun-
beams." The production was not, however, an unqualified success. After the first act there was a
threatened strike among the principal singers, which
was only averted by the Emperor's intervention. In
the opera-house the public demeanour was
enthusiastic enough, but outside there were, as
usual, jealous rivals of the composer working with
no small success to belittle his achievements and
diminish his profits. Indeed, he was so discouraged
by the reception of *Figaro* that he resolved never
to produce an opera in Vienna again. In Prague,
which, at the invitation of his friend Count Thun,
he visited in the following winter, there was a very
different spirit abroad. The Bohemians had taken
Figaro to their hearts. For weeks on end it filled
the opera-house with excited crowds; its tunes,
turned into waltzes or country dances, set every
foot in Prague a-jigging; and the blind fiddler at
the tavern door must needs strike up "Non più
andrai" if he would attract an audience or earn
a kreutzer. On the night of Mozart's arrival in
the town, his host took him to the theatre, where,
as usual, the favourite opera was being given. The
news quickly spread that the composer was in the
house, and, as the overture ended, the audience
rose like one man and cheered him to the echo. A
few days later he was persuaded to give a public
concert in the opera-house. The programme contained nothing but his own music, and it ended,
in response to insistent demands, with his playing
of a set of improvised variations on the most famous
of the airs in *Figaro*.

The kindly warmth of Prague's welcome
delighted Mozart, and he told the theatre man-

ager, Bondini, that as the Bohemians understood him so well he must write an opera on purpose for them. Bondini took him at his word, and there and then made a contract with him, at a substantial fee, to produce an opera for the next winter season. Mozart returned to Vienna in the spring of 1787, and once again sought the co-operation of Da Ponte in his new venture. This time it was the poet who was ready with a suggestion; he offered to write a libretto on the famous legend of Don Juan, and it should be called, "Il dissoluto punito ossia il Don Giovanni." The romantic subject, so rich in dramatic effectiveness, set Mozart's imagination aflame. Through the summer months, as he brooded over the story, the immortal music that was to adorn Da Ponte's text took shape in his mind, and when, in September, he set off on a second expedition to Prague, though not a note had been written down, the creation of *Don Giovanni* had been accomplished. Then for a few weeks he worked at the manuscript, sitting out in the garden of his friend, Franz Duschek, with a view of the old town lying below in the quiet autumn sunshine; by the middle of October the opera was ready for rehearsal, and the 29th of that month was fixed for the first performance. On the night before, there was a festive gathering at the Duscheks' house; Mozart was there, care-free and happy, delighting the company with his piano-playing, and trying over with his hostess the fine scena he had just composed for her. A friend gently reminded him that in twenty-four hours the curtain would be going up on *Don Giovanni,* and he had not yet written the overture. Quite unperturbed he went up to his room, and asked his wife to brew him a bowl of punch and to tell him fairy-tales while he worked at the overture. The fairy-tales kept him awake, but the punch induced drowsiness, and the night passed in alternating periods of sleep and feverish activity. By daybreak the score was finished and ready for the copyists to work on. So runs the engaging little tale, as Constanze told it many years afterwards; and she was even bold enough to suggest that some people would recognize in the music of the overture the " dosings and rousings " amid which it was composed. At any rate we may well believe that there was no time left for rehearsal, and that Mozart paid the excellent Prague orchestra the compliment of asking them to play the new overture at sight—a test which, by his own account, they passed with great credit, "although a good many notes certainly fell under the desks." The performance as a whole was a brilliant success for everyone concerned, it was repeated three times in the same week, and Guardasoni, the stage-manager, told Da Ponte that as long as he and Mozart lived the Prague opera-house need never fear a bad season.

In contrast to all this enthusiasm Mozart found the atmosphere of Vienna, whither he returned in the middle of November, decidedly chilling. Salieri's jealousy had been aroused by the news of his rival's triumph at Prague, and in his anxiety for the success of his own new opera, then just about to be produced, he did his best to prevent *Don Giovanni* from being heard in Vienna at all. It was not, in fact, performed there till May 1788, and then only by express command of the friendly Emperor Joseph. The eminent singers engaged, among whom was Mozart's first love, Aloysia Lange, in the part of Donna Anna, gave a good deal of trouble by demanding new songs to show off their voices better, and, to make room for these, the long-suffering composer had to rearrange some

of the scenes and cut out a large part of the last
finale. Even so the opera failed to please the
Viennese public; the critics charged it with being
too learned—" too crowded with effects of scienti-
fic harmony "—and after a few languid performances it disappeared from the repertory until
several years after the composer's death. Truly had
Mozart said of *Don Giovanni* that it was written a
little for Prague, not at all for Vienna, and most
of all for himself.

The third and last of the operas in which Da
Ponte collaborated with Mozart was *Così fan tutte,*
which was produced in Vienna in January, 1790.
This was written on a commission from the
Emperor, given only a few months before his death,
the last of his kindly acts to Mozart. Its plot—
said to be based on a recent scandalous episode in
Viennese social life—is absurd enough, and the
characters are in the highest degree unreal and
artificial, moving in the world described by Charles
Lamb—" The Utopia of gallantry, where pleasure
is duty and the manners perfect freedom." It was
the occasion, nevertheless, for Da Ponte to produce
his neatest and wittiest verse, and Mozart his most
enchanting music—music, it is true, in lighter vein
and of simpler texture than in the other great
comedies, but showing even more signally than they
the hand of an assured master of dramatic style.

CHAPTER XIII

Financial troubles—three great symphonies—visit to King of Prussia in Berlin—Leipzig—falling off in productive power.

To Mozart's nature there were two strongly contrasted sides. His artistic life was from the beginning under perfect control; he learnt by long and laborious study to bring his exuberant inventive faculty under the bracing discipline of exact form, and the very neatness of his manuscript scores reflects the orderly working of his mind. In practical affairs, on the other hand, he was careless and undisciplined to a degree. His life with Constanze in Vienna was from the first beset with financial troubles; only six months after his marriage we find him writing to Baroness von Waldstädten for money " to save his good name and his honour," and as the years went on his appeals to friends for loans to satisfy his creditors became more and more insistent. His position was no doubt a difficult one. With an uncertain income dependent on lesson-giving and the fickle favours of concert audiences, with the heavy expenses of his wife's continual ill health and frequent child-bearing (six children were born in nine years), there was obvious need for the most careful husbanding of resources. Mozart, thoughtlessly generous to anyone, friend or enemy, who seemed to be in need, incapable of making a businesslike arrangement with publisher or impresario or of securing that the profits from his compositions should not fall into other people's pockets, was singularly ill fitted to cope with such a situation. His wife, looking back in after years on her life with him in Vienna from the security of a prosperous second marriage, pictured herself as the patient martyr suffering from the thoughtlessness and extravagance of a man of genius who in practical affairs remained a child to the end of his days. She seems, however, to have done little herself to curb his extravagance or to assist his occasional efforts to economize. In 1784, the year in which Mozart started the thematic catalogue of his works, he began also to keep a meticulously exact record of his income and expenditure. The catalogue was kept up to the end, but the account-book, after a year, was handed over to Constanze and the entries soon ceased.

Mozart's long-delayed appointment to an official post at the Court in the latter part of 1787, accompanied though it was by a vague promise of further favours to come, did little to relieve his financial embarrassment. His salary as Kammermusikus to the Emperor was barely enough to pay for the rent of his lodgings, and for this he was required to turn out an endless supply of minuets and waltzes for the masked balls at the palace. "Too much for what I do, too little for what I could do," was the note he attached to the receipt for the first instalment. Yet it was long before he allowed his troubles and disappointments to damp his spirits or hamper his creative activity. In a few weeks of the summer of 1788 the poor dance composer gave to the world the three symphonies which are among its richest treasures. In these great works, strongly contrasted in mood but bound together by the perfection of artistic finish common to them all, the essential Mozart was revealed; and the glowing counterpoint at the climax of the " Jupiter " seemed to proclaim the assured triumph of his spirit over all earthly ills.

In the spring of 1789 one of Mozart's pupils, Prince von Lichnowsky, offered to take him on a visit to Berlin and to introduce him to the notice of King Frederick William of Prussia. The prospect of temporary escape from domestic worries, and of finding a new and possibly more generous patron than the master he was serving in Vienna, was certainly attractive, and he set out in the journey in high spirits. In Berlin he received the friendliest of welcomes from the King, who was a keen musical amateur and had heard enough of Mozart's fame to make him anxious that his visitor should get a favourable impression of the artistic accomplishments of his Court. So he entertained him with frequent performances by his private band and invited him to join select groups of his best players in string quartet practice. Asked by the King what he thought of the royal orchestra, Mozart replied with characteristic candour that His Majesty had the greatest assemblage of fine players in the world, but that if the gentlemen would keep together they might make better music. This frankness delighted Frederick William, and he at once suggested that Mozart should stay with him and, for a substantial salary, undertake the task of licking his orchestra into shape. It was a tempting offer, but Mozart, with the thought of the duty he owed to his good Emperor, hesitated to accept it; he must think the matter over before deciding.

On his way back to Vienna he paid a visit to Leipzig, where his friend Doles, once a pupil of J. S. Bach, had succeeded his master as cantor of the Thomasschule. Doles took him one day to play on the organ of St. Thomas's Church, where was enshrined the memory of a genius even greater than Mozart's, and as he listened to his masterly improvisation he said he could have believed old Bach to have risen from the grave. He was able also to show his friend some treasured relics of the great master—the eight-part motets—and to arrange for a performance of " Singet dem Herrn " by the pupils of his school. Mozart listened to the music with evident delight; then he asked to see the full score of the motet. Only the separate parts were available, so these he spread out on his knees and on the chairs around him and studied them long and earnestly till the whole work was absorbed in his mind.

The incident reminds us of the strange way in which the world treated the music of its greatest composer. For nearly a century after Bach's death the great bulk of his work was entirely neglected and unknown to all but a handful of enthusiasts. Mozart, towards the end of his life, as we have seen, obtained some access to the rich storehouse, but, even so, there is no evidence that he had any acquaintance with such acknowledged masterpieces as the *St. Matthew Passion* or the *B Minor Mass*. To him, as to most of his contemporaries, what is now the Bible of every music-lover was still a closed book.

On his return to Vienna at the beginning of June, Mozart made up his mind to decline the King of Prussia's offer. He was loth to leave the service of the kindly Emperor to whom he was genuinely attached, and even with the prospect of a comfortable salary and immediate relief from the harassing cares that pressed upon him, he could not bring himself to exchange the gaiety and freedom of Viennese life for the cold unfamiliar northern capital. But he was grateful for the King's kindness, and set to work at once on a set of string quartets that he had promised to write for him, and some piano sonatas for the Princess Frederica. In these there are signs for the first time of an impairment of productive power which the strain of incessant work and the long struggle with poverty combined to bring about. The quartets have not the spontaneous charm which marked the six dedicated to Haydn; the very appearance of the manuscripts, so far less neat and orderly than in the earlier works, seems to speak of an overtaxed brain and a troubled spirit. The bloom of his happiness was passing. The novelty of his piano-playing had worn off with the fickle Vienna audiences, the number of his pupils had dwindled almost to vanishing-point, and as his family increased and his carelessness remained untutored, his financial position grew steadily worse. Hopes of advancement at the Court were finally extinguished by the death, early in 1790, of Joseph II and the succession of an Emperor who cared little for music and who was disposed to regard with disfavour anyone who had enjoyed the protection of his predecessor. So it was that in the years 1789 and 1790 Mozart produced little that added to his reputation, and he occupied much of the time that in happier days he would have given to original work with the revision and enrichment of another man's music—the *Messiah* and other oratorios of Handel. Yet we owe to this barren period at least one gem of the purest ray—the quintet for clarinet and strings written in the autumn of 1789: the instrument that he had specially loved ever since he first heard it at Mannheim seemed to call the old spirit to life again.

CHAPTER XIV

Concert tour in German towns—the last year—*Die Zauberflöte*—commission to compose *Requiem*—*La Clemenza di Tito*—illness—death—*Requiem* left unfinished.

In the autumn of 1790 Mozart made one more effort to restore his fallen fortunes. There was clearly nothing to be hoped for in Vienna now that a new and unsympathetic Emperor was on the throne and the musical public had grown cold and indifferent; but there were other towns, surely, where his fame as a virtuoso could yet be turned to profitable account. So he set out on a concert tour, first to Frankfort, which seemed a promising field, as it was thronged just them with a large concourse for the festivities attending the election of Leopold II; then to Mannheim and Munich, scenes full of the memories, bitter and sweet, of his youthful years. To raise funds for the expenses of the journey poor Constanze had to part with most of the valuables she possessed, with little prospect, as she soon realized, of ever being able to redeem them. Mozart's letters to her while he was away were full of the old jokes and affectionate banter, but there was an undertone of anxious foreboding and sometimes tear-drops blotted the page. The proceeds of the tour were meagre in the extreme, and he returned home in early December to find his domestic affairs even worse than he had left them. Now, as the shadows deepened, he began to seek transient relief from his troubles by indulgence in the coarser pleasures of social life. There was no lack of companions to assist him in the congenial business of drowning his cares; his sister-in-law, Sophie Haibl, described him at this time as surrounded by " false friends, blood-suckers, and worthless people," whose only concern was to keep him amused at the supper-table. Stadler, the clarinet player, was the worst of these false friends. Mozart admired his talents, and not only composed masterpieces for his benefit but more than once helped him with gifts of money; yet the man repaid this generosity by playing the part of dishonest broker in the transactions for the recovery of Constanze's pawned trinkets.

The year 1791 was the last and most memorable of Mozart's short life. Now once more, after a barren interval, his inspiration returned in full flood, and before death struck him down he had given to the world works of a rare, almost unearthly beauty, in which he seemed to be exploring new regions and reaching forward to heights hitherto unscaled.

Both of the last masterpieces—*Die Zauberflöte* and the *Requiem*—had curious origins. There was prominent among the boon companions of Mozart's later years one Emanuel Schikaneder, who, after starting life as an itinerant fiddler, had taken to acting, and was now running a theatrical company of his own in a ramshackle building in the outskirts of Vienna. He had no education, but he was quick-witted and enterprising, popular with his subordinates, and a very shrewd judge of the kind of entertainment that was most likely to suit the popular taste. After the collapse of the Emperor's effort to establish a German theatre in Vienna, Italian opera had resumed its sway, but the people's taste for dramatic entertainments in

8

their native tongue had not been extinguished, and Schikaneder set himself to supply and stimulate this demand. He found, after various experiments, that what drew the largest audiences were musical pieces based on romantic fairy-tales, with an Oriental setting, startling scenic effects, and the special attraction of a whole menagerie of animals brought on the stage. It was with the offer of a libretto of this kind that he approached Mozart. The plot of the opera was to be of the conventional type, with a good fairy, a cruel magician, and a pair of lovers, who, after various adversities, were happily united in the end through the agency of a musical instrument of magical properties; and there was to be a good part with popular songs for the actor-manager that would enable him to display his talents as comedian to the best advantage. Mozart accepted the commission with some misgiving. He warned Schikaneder that he had never before tried his hand at music for a magic play and the result might well be a fiasco; but he was anxious to oblige a fellow Freemason; he had long been eager to help on the cause of German opera, and the chance now presented to him was at any rate better than none. So he set to work on *The Magic Flute*. Schikaneder provided him with a summer-house in the courtyard of his theatre, where he could work with the manager's eye upon him, and in the evenings, he induced the composer to seek relief from the labours of the day by joining him in riotous drinking bouts and other low forms of dissipation. Constanze was during these months away at Baden taking the waters, and her husband, left alone without even a servant to look after him, yielded only too readily to the temptations in his path.

The composition of the new opera pursued a

strangely chequered course. Less than half the music had been written when Schikaneder decided that the plot must be entirely changed; the wicked magician was to be made virtuous, the Queen of Night wicked, and a musical fairy-tale was to be converted into a glorification of Freemasonry. Mozart was probably a consenting party to this transformation—he may even have suggested it— though the recasting of the musical setting that it involved must have been a troublesome business. He had for some time been an ardent Freemason, and now, with the growing consciousness that the end of his earthly life was near, he was turning with a new devotion to the Masonic teaching about death and the hereafter for consolation and refreshment.

The revision of the opera resulted in an astonishing conglomeration. Side by side with the solemnities of Masonic ritual, introduced under the guise of the mysteries of Isis, and with the moral sentiments of Masonic philosophy sprinkled freely over the text, there were the buffooneries of the purely comic characters, and all the spectacular effects of a gorgeous pantomime. To produce an operatic masterpiece out of such material was only possible to one "whose head was in the heavens but whose feet were firmly planted on the stage." The difficulties of Mozart's task, moreover, were seriously increased by two commissions that came to him while he was engaged upon it. One day in July a stranger called on him, with an anonymous letter inviting him to compose a Requiem Mass : he was not to inquire as to the source from which the commission came, but he could name his own price for the work. The offer had a peculiar attraction for Mozart, and he had no wish to ask inconvenient questions before accepting it. It was long

since he had written any music for the service of
the Church, and he was anxious to show once more
what he could do in this branch of the art. Moreover the commission seemed to come to him with a
kind of spiritual authority; it was a voice from the
unseen world, whose summons he could not refuse
to obey. It had, in fact, no such exalted origin.
The mysterious messenger was the steward of a
certain Count Walsegg, a wealthy musical amateur,
who, with the object of gaining fame as a composer, adapted the simple expedient of giving
anonymous commissions to eminent persons to
write works for him that he could pass as his own;
these he paid for liberally, and in due course had
them performed under his name. Just now he was
anxious to honour the memory of his dead wife,
and it occurred to him that a Requiem from
Mozart's pen would provide him with effective
material for this purpose.

The other interruption of the composer's work
on *The Magic Flute* came, a month later, from
Prague. There the coronation of the Emperor
Leopold as King of Bohemia was to take place on
September 6th, and at the last moment the authorities decided to celebrate it with a new opera by
Mozart. It was to be an *opera seria* in a form
already obsolete, of which *Idomeneo* had been a
notable specimen; an old libretto of Metastasio's—
La Clemenza di Tito—based on a dull story of
ancient Rome, was unearthed and remodelled for
the occasion, and Mozart was allowed less than a
month to provide the musical setting. He set out at
once for Prague with his wife and his pupil, Süssmayer, in a state of severe nervous agitation, which
was increased by the sudden reappearance at
that moment of Count Walsegg's messenger with
urgent inquiries as to the progress of the promised

Requiem. Composition had to be done in his carriage on the road, and wherever he stopped for a night's lodging his ideas were put into writing with the assistance of the faithful Süssmayer. In this way the opera was actually completed in eighteen days. The conditions under which it was written were hardly favourable for the creation of a masterpiece, and though its performance on the night of the coronation banquet was on a scale of lavish splendour, nothing could conceal the perfunctory and uninspired quality of the music. Weary and disappointed, Mozart returned to Vienna. Constanze resumed her cure at Baden but by this time her husband was more in need of medical treatment than she. The dissipation into which Schikaneder led him had undermined his strength, and to this there was added the strain of work at high pressure on the Prague opera and mortification at its subsequent failure. But *The Magic Flute* had to be finished somehow, and by a desperate effort Mozart managed to get it ready for performance by the last day of September. On the opening night the first act was rather coldly received, and the composer, in a state of gloom and agitation, went behind the scenes in the interval to seek reassurance from Schikaneder, who was playing the part of Papageno. The manager was quite undismayed, and cheerfully expressed his entire confidence in the ultimate success of the piece. His optimism was thoroughly justified. The beauties of the latter part of the opera soon dispelled the apathy of the audience, and at each subsequent performance, with the attraction of some additional comic business provided for Papageno, there was a steady crescendo of popular enthusiasm. Schikaneder had evidently struck a gold-mine in *The Magic Flute,* and through the month of October he gave it at his theatre nearly every night. It filled the manager's pockets, but no appreciable share of the profits found its way into the composer's. For this shabby treatment Mozart enjoyed at least a posthumous compensation in the special favour shown to his masterpiece by two men of outstanding genius. Beethoven pronounced it to be the greatest of all Mozart's operas, and Goethe esteemed it so highly that during the years in which he directed the Weimar theatre he had it performed no less than eighty-two times. He even began to write a sequel to it, and, though this was never finished, the influence of *The Magic Flute* on the poet's mind can clearly be traced in the Second Part of *Faust*.

With his opera now fairly launched on the tide of success, Mozart resumed work on the *Requiem* with feverish intensity. Morbid imaginings began to crowd in upon him. He was continually haunted by the vision of the messenger of death from the unseen world; he believed that he had been poisoned, and now it seemed that he was writing a Requiem for his own obsequies. To a friend who proposed to take him on a visit to England he sent a pathetic letter to explain why he must refuse the very plan that he had long wished to carry out. " I feel stunned," he wrote; " I reason with difficulty . . . I go on writing because composition tires me less than resting. I know from what I suffer that the hour has come. I am at the point of death—I have come to an end before having had the enjoyment of my talent. Life was indeed so beautiful . . . my career began under such happy auspices; but one cannot change one's own destiny . . . It will be as Providence wills, and so I finish my death-song. I must not leave it incomplete."

When Constanze returned home she found him in an alarming state of weakness and depression. She at once called in a doctor, and instisted on taking the score of the *Requiem* away from him. But the tireless brain could not rest. He responded instantly to a request from his Masonic Lodge that he should compose a cantata to be sung at their coming festival, and, with his thoughts set in a new direction, the cloud of depression lifted for a time. He finished the music, and was well enough to conduct a performance of the cantata on November 15th, but two days later he had a serious relapse, and it was evident that the end was near. Day after day he struggled on with the *Requiem*, sometimes dictating to Süssmayer as the music took final shape in his mind, or showing him in rough outline his ideas for the later numbers that had still to be written; and in the evenings when he was told that *The Magic Flute* was being given at Schikaneder's theatre he would follow the performance in imagination, with a watch by his bedside. On the 4th of December he asked that some of his friends might come and try through the vocal parts of the *Requiem* with him. A quartet of singers was formed, with the composer himself taking alto part. They had got as far as the *Lacrymosa* when there was an abrupt stop. Mozart, with the sudden realization that the work could never be finished, burst into tears, and thrust the score away from him. Then he turned to his wife, and said: " I have the taste of death on my tongue. Did I not tell you that I was writing the *Requiem* for myself? But I should like to hear my *Magic Flute* once more," and he began to hum the birdcatcher's song. One of the friends, sitting at his bedside, went to the piano and sang the song—to Mozart's evident delight. So in the early morning hours of the 5th of December, with one of his own lovely tunes ringing in his ears, he passed to his rest.

The immediate cause of death was typhus, and it is possible that the malignant character of the disease made it necessary that interment should take place with the least possible delay. But it is difficult to excuse the conduct of Baron von Swieten, who took over from the stricken and helpless Constanze the duty of arranging the last rites, and who thought fit to dishonour his friend's memory by the indignity of a pauper's funeral. On the afternoon of the 5th of December, the body was hurriedly taken to the public cemetery. On the way a violent storm of rain and sleet broke out; the little company of mourners refused to go further, no friend stood by to see the coffin lowered into the common vault, and no mark was left to distinguish the grave of Mozart from that of the beggars around him.

It remains to tell the strange story of the *Requiem* to its end. The composer had left the earlier part of the Mass as perfectly finished as anything that came from his pen, but of the last few numbers there remained nothing but some rough sketches and so much as Süssmayer could recollect of his master's last instructions. With this material, Süssmayer undertook the task of completing the score of the *Requiem*. How much of the music of the disputed numbers was his handiwork must always remain uncertain. Probably the greater part of it was nothing more than a filling-in of the outline left by Mozart, or an incorporation of the musical ideas that the master had discussed with his pupil. In any case the job was undoubtedly executed with considerable skill; it was as a finished work of art that the *Requiem* was finally delivered into the hands of Count Walsegg's messenger. A year or two later the Count himself directed a performance of the work, with no suggestion that the music came from any other hand than his own!

Mozart died young—with his thirty-sixth year not yet completed—as was fitting for one whom the gods loved, the gods who " *approve*

> *The depth, and not the tumult, of the soul,*
> *A fervent, not ungovernable, love."*

During the last months of his life there had come a favourable turn in his fortunes. The offer of the post of Kapellmeister to the cathedral of St. Stephen, with substantial emoluments, and commissions from Holland and Hungary for the regular supply of musical works, promised relief from the financial cares that had so long pressed upon him. But it was too late. " I must go," he said, " just when I should have been able to live in peace. I must leave my art when, no longer the slave of fashion nor the tool of speculators, I could follow the dictates of my own feeling and write whatever my heart prompts." So, perhaps, it might have been. It is possible that with a longer span of life, set free from gnawing anxiety, and able to garner in peace the fruits of a deeper experience, his genius would have soared to even greater heights than those it had already attained. But in the best of Mozart's music as he left it there are all the marks of final and victorious achievement. It has the dewy freshness of spring, the clean-limbed strength of young manhood; and we may well be content to know that he who created it for the world's delight was not allowed to grow old.

SELECT BIBLIOGRAPHY

Grove's *Dictionary of Music and Musicians*—article "Mozart."

Oxford History of Music; Vol. V., " The Viennese Period," by W. H. Hadow.

O. Jahn: *Wolfgang Amadeus Mozart.*

T. de Wyzewa and G. de Saint-Foix: *W. A. Mozart, sa vie musicale et son œuvre.*

A. Schurig: *Wolfgang Amadeus Mozart.*

H. Rau: *Mozart—Ein Künstlerleben.*

L. Schiedermair: *Die Briefe Mozarts und seiner Familie.*

Lady Wallace: *The Letters of W. A. Mozart translated, from the collection of L. Nohl.*

E. Holmes: *Life of Mozart.*

Barrington's *Miscellanies.*

Michael Kelly's *Reminiscences.*

Da Ponte's *Memoirs.*

Burney: *Present State of Music in France and Italy.*

E. J. Dent: *Mozart's Operas.*

Eric Blom: *Mozart* (Master Musicians' Series).

A. Einstein: *Mozart—His Character, His Work.*

SELECT LIST OF MOZART'S WORKS

Köchel's *Verzeichnis* (3rd edition 1937) is the standard classification of Mozart's works by dates and themes. The K-numbers given below are taken from this classification.

K.38	*Apollo and Hyacinthus.*
K.50	*Bastien and Bastienne.* Opera. 1768.
K.51	*La Finta Semplice.* Comic Opera. 1768.
K.80	String Quartet in G. 1770.
K.87	*Mitridate.* Opera. 1770.
K.99	Cassation in B flat. 1769.
K.126	*Scipio's Dream.* Masque. 1772.
K.135	*Lucio Silla.* Opera. 1772.
K.155–160	String Quartets in D, G, F, B flat and E flat. 1772.
K.165	*Exsultate, Jubilate.* Motet for Soprano. 1773.
K.168–173	String Quartets in F, A, C, E flat, B flat and D minor. 1773.
K.174	String Quintet in B flat. 1773.
K.175	Piano Concerto in D. 1773.
K.183	Symphony in G minor. 1773.
K.196	*La Finta Giardiniera.* Comic Opera. 1774.
K.200	Symphony in C. 1773.
K.201	Symphony in A. 1774.
K.207	Violin Concerto in B flat. 1775.
K.208	*Il Rè Pastore.* Masque. 1775.
K.211, 216 –218, 219	Violin Concertos in D, G, D and A. 1775.
K.238	Piano Concerto in B flat. 1776.
K.246	Piano Concerto in C. 1776.
K.247	Divertimento for Strings and Horns in F. 1776.
K.250	Serenade in D ("Haffner"). 1776.
K.271	Piano Concerto in E flat. 1777.
K.274–284	Piano Sonatas in C, F, B flat, E flat, G and D. 1774–5.
K.287	Divertimento for Strings and Horns in B flat. 1777.
K.297	Symphony in D ("Paris"). 1778.
K.299	Flute and Harp Concerto in C. 1778.
K.301–306	Violin Sonatas in G, E flat, C, E minor, A and D. 1777–8.
K.309–311	Piano Sonatas in C, A minor and D. 1777–8.
K.313	Flute Concerto in G. 1778.
K.319	Symphony in B flat. 1779.
K.330–333	Piano Sonatas in C, A, F and B flat. 1778.
K.334	Divertimento for Strings and Horns in D. 1779.
K.538	Symphony in C. 1780.
K.350	*Schlafe, Mein Prinzchen.* Song. (Spurious).

K.358	Piano Sonata for four hands in B flat. 1774.
K.361	Serenade for 13 wind instruments in B flat. 1781.
K.364	Sinfonia Concertante for Violin and Viola in E flat. 1779.
K.365	Two Piano Concerto in E flat. 1779.
K.366	*Idomeneo.* Opera. 1780.
K.375	Serenade for wind instruments in E flat. 1781.
K.376–380	Violin Sonatas in E, F, B flat, G and E flat. 1781.
K.381	Piano Sonata for four hands in D. 1772.
K.384	*Il Seraglio.* Opera. 1782.
K.385	Symphony in D ("Haffner"). 1782.
K.387	String Quartet in G. 1783.
K.388	Serenade for wind instruments in C minor. 1782.
K.402, 403	Violin Sonatas in A and C. 1782.
K.413–415	Piano Concertos in F, A and C. 1782–3.
K.421	String Quartet in D minor. 1783.
K.422	*L'Oca del Cairo.* Comic Opera (unfinished). 1783.
K.425	Symphony in C ("Linz"). 1783.
K.427	Mass in C minor. 1783.
K.428	String Quartet in E flat. 1783.
K.442	Trio in D. 1783.
K.448	Two Piano Sonata in D. 1781.
K.449–451	Piano Concertos in E flat, B flat and D. 1783–4.
K.453	Piano Concerto in G. 1784.
K.454	Violin Sonata in B flat. 1784.
K.456	Piano Concerto in B flat. 1784.
K.457	Piano Sonata in C minor. 1784.
K.458	String Quartet in B flat ("Hunt"). 1784.
K.459	Piano Concerto in F. 1784.
K.464, 465	String Quartets in A and C. 1784.
K.466, 467	Piano Concertos in D minor and C. 1784–5.
K.475	Piano Fantasia in C minor. 1784.
K.481	Violin Sonata in E flat. 1785.
K.482	Piano Concerto in E flat. 1785.
K.486	*The Impresario.* Comic Opera. 1786.
K.488	Piano Concerto in A. 1786.
K.491	Piano Concerto in C minor. 1786.
K.492	*The Marriage of Figaro.* Comic Opera. 1786.
K.496	Trio in G. 1786.
K.497	Piano Sonata for four hands. 1786.
K.499	String Quartet in D ("Hoffmeister"). 1786.
K.502	Trio in B flat. 1786.
K.503	Piano Concerto in C. 1786.
K.504	Symphony in D ("Prague"). 1786.
K.515, 516	String Quintets in C and G minor. 1787–8.
K.521	Piano Sonata for four hands in C. 1787.

K.522	*A Musical Joke.* Divertimento in F. 1787.
K.525	Serenade for Strings in G ("Eine kleine Nachtmusik"). 1787.
K.526	Violin Sonata in A. 1787.
K.527	*Don Giovanni.* Comic Opera. 1787.
K.537	Piano Concerto in D ("Coronation"). 1788.
K.542	Trio in E. 1788.
K.543	Symphony in E flat. 1788.
K.545	Piano Sonata in C ("for Beginners"). 1788.
K.548	Trio in C. 1788.
K.550	Symphony in G minor. 1788.
K.551	Symphony in C ("Jupiter"). 1788.
K.564	Trio in G. 1788.
K.570	Piano Sonata in B flat. 1789.
K.572	Orchestration of Handel's *Messiah.* 1789.
K.575	String Quartet in D. 1789.
K.576	Piano Sonata in D. 1789.
K.581	Quintet for Clarinet and Strings in A ("Stadler"). 1789.
K.588	*Così fan Tutte.* Comic Opera. 1789.
K.589, 590	String Quartets in B flat and F. 1789.
K.593	String Quintet in D. 1790.
K.595	Piano Concerto in B flat. 1790–1.
K.614	String Quintet in E flat. 1791.
K.618	*Ave Verum Corpus.* Motet. 1791.
K.620	*The Magic Flute.* Opera. 1791.
K.621	*La Clemenza di Tito.* Opera. 1791.
K.626	*Requiem* (unfinished). 1791.